SUNDAY TELEGRAPH

101
WAYS OF
SAVING TAX

D1789400

SUNDAY TELEGRAPH

101
WAYS OF

SAVING TAX

BILL PACKER
△ Touche Ross

Published by Telegraph Publications
135 Fleet Street, London EC4P 4BL

First published April 1982
© Touche Ross & Co. 1982
Second edition, updated, March 1983
Third edition completely revised, March 1984
Fourth edition updated and revised, March 1985
Fifth edition updated and revised, March 1986
Sixth edition updated and revised, March 1987
ISBN 0 86367 109 8

Packer, Bill
   101 ways of saving tax. – 6th ed.
   1. Tax planning – Great Britain
   2. Taxation – Law and legislation – Great Britain
   I. Title
   344.1034   KD5370

ISBN 0-8637-109-8

Design Stephen Lang
Typeset by BSC Print Ltd.
Printed in Great Britain by Biddles Ltd.

Acknowledgement

Bill Packer would like to record his thanks to Elaine Baker, whose original concept this book was and who contributed much of the initial material.

Preface

There are a number of tax guides on the market, but none so clear and concise as this *Sunday Telegraph* publication which has proved a great success in the seven years it has been published. Every year the tax regime appears to get more complicated and every year the need for simple and intelligent advice becomes more pressing. Our growing mailbag of readers' letters in the City office of the *Sunday Telegraph* bears witness to the keen interest that everyone has in the amount of tax they pay.

Unlike other books, this one is aimed at showing you ways to cut your tax bill, not through complex schemes but by straightforward savings in areas which may perhaps be neglected by even quite financially sophisticated people.

It has been written as before by Bill Packer of Touche Ross, who has done wonders in simplifying some esoteric subjects into an easily understandable text.

The Chancellor of the Exchequer's 1987 March Budget was a marvel of brevity and caution, while managing to cut the basic rate of income tax to 27p in the pound (from 29p), at a cost to the Exchequer of some £2 billion. This book contains all the relevant Budget changes, including such areas as inheritance tax and pensions. It provides the reader with an up-to-date and highly efficient compass to steer him (or her) through the maze of the tax system.

New readers should ensure that this book becomes a required adjunct to their financial affairs–just as it has for the many readers who have benefited from this expert advice since it was first published in 1981.

Alex Murray, City Editor, March 1987

CONTENTS

The text includes the changes announced in the Budget on 17th March 1987. These may be amended before the 1987 Finance Act becomes law, probably at the beginning of August 1987. You should therefore check the position if you think you may be affected by the current Budget proposals.

1 BASIC QUESTIONS FOR THE INDIVIDUAL (Income Tax)

2 YOU HAVE EARNED IT (Taxation of the Employee)

3 NOW YOU ARE IN BUSINESS (Taxation of the Self-employed)

4 KEEPING GOOD COMPANY (Taxation of the Company – Corporation Tax)

5 SOME YOU WIN–SOME YOU LOSE (Capital Gains Tax and the Individual)

6 CAPITAL WAYS OF SAVING TAX (Inheritance Tax)

7 THE INDIRECT TAX YOU MUST PAY (Value Added Tax)

9 RANGE OF POSSIBILITIES

1 BASIC QUESTIONS FOR THE INDIVIDUAL

INCOME TAX

1   Do I have to pay tax? If so, how much will I have to pay? ●

You may be amused to learn that, in theory, income tax is only a temporary measure; it has to be renewed by Parliament each year, and will cease to be imposed by Parliament when the country no longer requires revenue to be raised in this manner! Income tax was first introduced in 1799 to pay for the Napoleonic wars, and was abolished after Waterloo, in 1816. In 1842, income tax was reintroduced by Sir Robert Peel, again as a temporary measure, but nearly a century and a half later income tax is still being paid!

As a starting point it is important that you understand what your *taxable income* is.

The total income of you, as an individual, should include income of both yourself and your wife (if applicable) from all sources whether earned or unearned. *Earned income* is income arising from any office or employment, the personal carrying-on of a trade, profession or vocation, pay or pension in respect of past services, and certain social security benefits. *Investment* (or *unearned*) income includes dividends plus tax credits, property income, interest from banks or building societies, annual payments, etc. (Note, these lists are not exhaustive.)

To arrive at your taxable income, from this total figure are deducted allowances, reliefs and charges on income (covered in later questions); the latter includes annual payments and interest paid which is allowable for tax purposes. Charges are normally deducted from investment income first, unless it is more advantageous for you to have the deduction from your earned income.

Having arrived at the figure of your taxable income, this is taxed according to the income tax rates for that particular year. A year, for income tax purposes, commences on *6th April*, so the references to the end of a tax year are to *5th April*, not 31st December. Thus the tax year *1986/87 runs from 6th April 1986 to 5th April 1987*. The rates applied to your taxable income for these two years are as follows:

Rate	1986/87 Taxable income	Rate	1987/88 Taxable income
%	£	%	£
29	1–17,200	27	1–17,900
40	17,201–20,200	40	17,901–20,400
45	20,201–25,400	45	20,401–25,400
50	25,401–33,300	50	25,401–33,300
55	33,301–41,200	55	33,301–41,200
60	over 41,200	60	over 41,200

The following example shows how the amount of taxable income is arrived at and how the tax is charged.

Example

Stan D. Easy is a retired army corporal and in the year 1986/87 he receives an annual pension of £3,000; he is now in part-time employment and receives a salary of £8,000 per annum. He holds shares in various companies and during the year ended 5th April 1987 he receives dividends plus tax credits of £3,500. He pays mortgage interest on his house of £1,650, and he is a married man–his wife's only income is interest from a bank account amounting to £75. His taxable income for 1986/87 was as follows.

	£
Salary	8,000
Pension	3,000
Dividends + tax credits	3,500
Bank interest (wife) (see question 19)	75
Total income	14,575
less Interest paid	1,650
	12,925
less Personal allowance (see question 6)	3,655
Taxable income	£ 9,270

This is charged to tax at 29%: £9,270 at 29% = £2,688.30 and this is Stan's total tax bill. From this figure is deducted all the tax he has paid and it is then possible to see whether he has paid too much or too little tax during the year, the balance being either collected from him or repaid to him (see also question 3).

On 18th March 1986 the Chancellor of the Exchequer published a Green Paper on 'The Reform of Personal Taxation' with the intention, after due consultation, of introducing far reaching changes to the existing system to take effect in 1990.

2   Is there any extra tax to pay on my investment income?

For tax years up to and including 1983/84, if your *unearned income* exceeded a specific limit, you would have had to pay an *investment income surcharge* of 15% on the excess of your unearned income over that limit, after allowing for certain deductions, in particular interest paid (see questions 17 and 18). For 1983/84, the limit was fixed at £7,100.

For 1984/85 and later years, the surcharge has been abolished.

Commonly, investment income is paid with income tax at the basic rate deducted or treated as deducted at source. If therefore you are liable to tax at higher rates it will be necessary for the Inspector of Taxes to issue a special assessment (known as a 'taxed income' assessment) to collect the additional liability. This additional tax is not due for payment until 1st December following the end of the year of assessment concerned, at the earliest: thus the additional liability for the year 1986/87 will not be due for payment until 1st December 1987. If the assessment is not issued in time for the 1st December due date then the tax becomes due 30 days after the notice of assessment is issued.

3   When and how do I pay the tax? What can I do if I disagree with the amount I am asked to pay?

Tax will be collected from you in one of two ways–either by *deduction at source* or by way of an *assessment* issued by the Inspector of Taxes, which informs you of the amount to pay direct to the Revenue.

The most common example of tax being deducted at source is if you are an employee–you will receive your weekly/monthly salary after tax and national insurance contributions have been deducted (see also question 27). On the other hand you may be a self-employed person, in which case there is no employer to deduct tax from your earnings during the tax year. Instead, you will send in accounts to the Inspector of Taxes showing details of your income and expenditure for the year, he will then issue an assessment on your taxable profit for the relevant tax year (see also questions 36 to 51). Unearned income is also taxed by assessment unless it is a very small amount, in which case part of your personal allowances will be used to cover the amount chargeable. There is yet another form of assessment, to collect higher rate tax due on investment income (see question 2). Finally, even if you are an employee you may receive an assessment (which will show income from employments and the tax deducted) after the end of the tax year if, for some reason, you have paid too much or too little tax, despite the regular deductions made by your employer (see question 28 for more details).

For whatever reason you receive an assessment you should always check to see if it is correct. If you have a professional adviser you should authorise him to receive a copy of all assessments issued to you. In case the copy does not reach your adviser, you should give him your own copy of the notice of assessment as soon as possible.

If you do not agree with the figures shown on the assessment you have 30 days in which to *appeal* against it, stating your reasons and whether or not you wish part, or all, of the tax charged to be withheld from collection until the figures have been agreed. The procedure for making an appeal or a request for postponement of the tax charged is covered in the notes which are always issued with a notice of assessment, but if you have a professional adviser he will deal with this for you.

If you appeal against an assessment on the grounds that it is estimated and the Inspector of Taxes is awaiting accounts or other details from you, you should not delay sending him the information. Indeed, should you fail to do this, he has the right to take you before an independent body called the General Commissioners who, when the facts are put before them, have the power to determine (or confirm) the assessment in whatever amount they consider appropriate, which almost inevitably leads to excessive tax having to be paid by you!

If you are self-employed you will normally pay the tax due in two equal instalments on *1st January* during the year of assessment and *1st July* immediately following the end of the year of assessment. For the year 1987/88 tax is payable on 1st January 1988 and 1st July 1988 (remembering that the year commences on 6th April 1987 and ends on 5th April 1988). If the assessment is issued too late to pay tax on these dates you will be given *30 days* to pay the tax.

If there is tax to pay on an assessment, *the notice will always state quite clearly the due date for payment of the tax. Remember* there is an *interest charge* (currently at 9.5% per annum) which accrues daily from what is called the *reckonable date* (which will vary depending on the circumstances) to the date payment of the tax is made.

You should not delay paying your tax after the due and payable date: it will benefit no-one, for you always run the risk of having an extra charge to pay–interest. If you incur an interest charge on overdue tax (of any description) it is not deductible for any tax purposes.

On the other hand, if the situation is reversed and the Inland Revenue owe you a refund of tax, there may be a *repayment supplement* due to you. Again, this is calculated at 9.5% per annum and will be paid to you provided certain tests concerning original due dates of payment of the tax are fulfilled.

There is one other area which concerns collection of tax. In 1971 the Revenue introduced a practice whereby they do not collect arrears of tax if this has arisen due to some error on their part involving failure to make proper and timely use of information relating to a taxpayer's income or personal circumstances.

The proportion of arrears forgiven in this way depends on the taxpayer's gross income and ranges from all the tax being forgiven if the gross income is less than £8,500 to all the arrears being collected if the income exceeds £23,000. (These limits are increased by £2,500 for pensioners.)

These cases are not that common and the Revenue looks at the circumstances very carefully before a case of 'official error' is admitted.

4   Can I save tax by keeping quiet?

A surprising number of people think that if they do not send in their income tax returns or trading accounts it will save them tax. There are also a number of people who omit, quite inadvertently, to make entries on their returns of income, or neglect to keep the Revenue informed of their circumstances. Finally, there are the people who deliberately withhold information from the Inland Revenue in the belief that no-one will ever know, and they have therefore 'got away with it'!

These people are, of course, quite wrong in their views–there is no excuse for withholding details of your income and gains from the Inland Revenue. Even if the Inspector fails to send you an income tax return for completion, this does not discharge you from your liability—you should inform him even if he does not ask. Be certain you are not misled into thinking 'the Inspector will never know'—the Revenue has extensive powers which are used to obtain information not only from you as an individual, but from many other sources.

The most common source from which the Revenue receives information is the banks and building societies which, by law, have to forward to the Revenue, details of interest credited to each person's deposit account where this exceeds a specified amount. This information is imparted to the individual's own tax office and checked with his return. . . the rest is obvious! This is just an example but in the larger cases of omissions from returns etc. there can be *interest charges* and *penalties,* in addition to the tax charged, possibly for many years of assessment.

The answer to this question, then, is most definitely—no. Instead of paying *less* tax you *may end up paying large amounts of tax in lump sums, penalties, interest* and possibly a *professional adviser's fees* if you employed someone to deal with your problems.

● **5 What is the basic personal allowance?**

For 1986/87 the *lower* personal allowance is £2,335; for 1987/88 it is £2,425. This will be granted if you are an unmarried person (whether single, divorced or widowed), and even if you are not entitled to claim any other allowances, this amount will be deducted from your income before the tax is calculated.

Legislation was introduced in 1980 for indexation of the main personal allowances (including this relief) so the amount of relief should be revised each tax year, by reference to any increase in the Retail Prices Index (RPI) during the 12 months to the previous December. The amounts of the increase are rounded up to the nearest £100.

● **6 Can I claim for my wife and children?**

There is a *higher* personal allowance due if you are a married man and your wife lives with you, or is wholly maintained by you. There are special rules for the year of marriage or separation (see questions 8 and 11). The relief for 1986/87 is £3,655 and for 1987/88 is £3,795.

Tax allowances in respect of children were generally abolished some years ago (but see question 12–single parent families). The allowances have been replaced by child benefits which are payable direct to the mother of the child by the Department of Health and Social Security normally through the Post Office or by credit transfer. These child benefits are not taxable.

It should be pointed out that the status of a common law wife is not recognised for tax purposes.

7   Are there any other personal allowances I can claim for myself or my family?

There are several other reliefs which you may be able to claim; these are noted below:

Dependent relatives: The dependant must be a relative who is maintained by the claimant, and must be incapacitated by old age or infirmity, unless she is the mother of the claimant, or his wife, when the only test is that she is widowed, divorced or separated. ('Relative' includes relatives of husband and wife.)

The allowance is £100 a year but this is increased to £145 for a woman claimant other than a married woman living with her husband. To obtain the full allowance the relative's income must not exceed the basic retirement pension for the year in question–the allowance is reduced by £1 for every £1 the relative's income exceeds the limit.

If the relative is not living with you, the allowance will be given, as a concession, if your contribution is £75 or more each year.

An allowance may be claimed for *each* dependent relative.

Daughter's or son's services: The daughter or son must be resident with the claimant and be maintained by him. He must be compelled to depend on these services because of old age or infirmity. The allowance is £55 a year.

Blind person's relief: This can be claimed by a single person or a married man if he (or his wife) is registered as blind throughout the whole or part of the year. If both spouses are blind, the allowance is given twice. For 1987/88 the allowance is £540 a year; for 1986/87 and earlier years it was £360.

Housekeeper allowance: A claim for this allowance (£100) can be made by a *widow* or *widower* but *not* by a person who is divorced or separated, in respect of a relative who is resident with the claimant, or an unrelated person who is resident and employed as a housekeeper. This is no longer a common relief because if there are children involved there is an additional personal allowance that may be claimed (see question 12).

Life assurance relief: For most life assurance policies issued up to and including 13th March 1984, income tax relief at 15% is allowed on the premiums paid. Normally the relief is given by means of a deduction by the payer from the premiums he pays, so that no intervention is required by the tax office.

The relief is not given on policies issued after 13th March 1984; it will also be withdrawn on any existing policies made before that date if the policy terms are altered so as to improve the benefits received.

The full list of personal allowances is given in Appendix 2.

● **8   What happens to my tax in the year of my marriage?**

As already mentioned under question 1, the income of husband and wife are normally treated as one and taxed accordingly. However, in the year of marriage, special rules apply.

At one time, the date of your wedding made a considerable difference to your tax for the year of marriage. Over the years the rules have progressively changed until they now operate as follows.

Husband: The married man's allowance is reduced by one-twelfth of the difference between the single and married man's allowances, for each month in the tax year which ended before his marriage (i.e. ending 5th May, 5th June, etc.).

Wife: The single person's allowance is given throughout the year of marriage and the wife is not treated as married until 6th April following the date of marriage (i.e. the start of the new tax year). At this point the wife's personal allowances disappear, though if she is working it is replaced by the *Wife's Earned Income Allowance* (see question 9).

9   If I am a working wife do I pay my own tax?

As you have already seen, if you are a married woman, for income tax purposes your income is *deemed to be that of your husband*. He must therefore declare all your income (whether it is earned or un-earned) on his income tax return and any assessments to be made on your income will be sent direct to him, unless an election has been made to the contrary (see question 10). Your husband is therefore liable to pay the income tax due on your joint incomes (except in special circumstances when the Revenue may require payment from you, or where an election has been made).

The exception to this is if you are employed and pay tax under PAYE. In this case the tax is deducted direct from your earnings and if at the end of the year you have paid too much tax, the repayment will be sent direct to you and not your husband.

As a working wife you will be granted a *Wife's Earned Income Allowance* which is the same as the single person's allowance (i.e. £2,335 for 1986/87, £2,425 for 1987/88); if you are self-employed this allowance will be given in the assessment (whether you are trading on your own or in partnership) and if you are employed, the allow-ance will form the basis for your coding (see questions 27 and 32). If your earnings are below the amount of the allowance the remainder of the relief has to be forfeited but, *if your husband's income is less than his total allowances, you may claim the excess allowances* against your own income.

Remember, this only works one way, the allowances are passed from husband to wife but *not* vice versa.

10   Can I be separately assessed from my husband? Do I have to pay my wife's tax?

These two questions must be dealt with together as the answers are related: *as the wife–yes,* you can be separately assessed from your husband, and *as the husband–no,* you do not always have to pay your wife's tax.

There are two forms of separate assessment and they must not be confused:

1 Separate taxation of wife's earnings: This is generally called Wife's Earnings Election and works in the following way. It has already been seen that the wife's income is assessed as an additional source of the husband's income and he will pay tax accordingly. If his earnings are very high he may have used up all the basic rate band (which taxes income at 27% in 1987/88, 29% in 1986/87) and the wife's income is therefore taxed at 40% or higher. However, the Wife's Earnings Election, *which must be made jointly by husband and wife* during the period from 6 months before until 12 months after the end of the relevant year of assessment, provides that the *wife's earned income becomes her own responsibility*. The husband continues to be assessed on his own income and any income of his wife which is unearned; he *forfeits the higher personal allowance* of a married man and receives only the single person's allowance. The wife is also taxed as a single person, receiving the lower personal allowance, but in this way *both parties receive the benefit of their own basic rate bands*.

Your joint earnings must be substantial to make a claim worthwhile, remembering that the husband will lose part of his allowances. You should certainly consider making an election if your joint earned income is in the region of £26,000 or more, but the precise level at which it would be advantageous for you personally to make such a claim must depend on your individual circumstances.

In some cases, the Revenue may advise you to make an election, or you should seek professional advice if you are not sure what to do. The election can be revoked, if both parties agree, up to 12 months after the end of the tax year to which the election no longer to apply.

Example

Paul Over is a director of a knitwear manufacturing company, and in the tax year 1986/87 he is paid a salary of £27,000 per annum. His wife Eileen D. Over is a keep-fit instructress earning a salary of £12,000 per annum.

Without Wife's Earnings Election tax is due as follows.

	Total £	Paul £	Eileen £
Salaries	39,000	27,000	12,000
less allowances:			
Married man's allowance	(3,655)	(3,655)	—
Wife's earned income allowance	(2,335)	—	(2,335)
	£33,010	£23,345	£9,665
Chargeable to tax:			
at 29%	17,200	17,200	—
at 40%	3,000	3,000	—
at 45%	5,200	3,145	2,055
at 50%	7,610	—	7,610
	£33,010	£23,345	£9,665
Tax payable:	£12,333	£7,603	£4,730

With Wife's Earnings Election tax is due as follows.

	£	£	£
Salary	39,000	27,000	12,000
less single person's allowance	(4,670)	(2,335)	(2,335)
	£34,330	£24,665	£9,665
Chargeable to tax:			
at 29%	26,865	17,200	9,665
at 40%	3,000	3,000	—
at 45%	4,465	4,465	—
	£34,330	£24,665	£9,665
Tax payable:	£11,000	£8,197	£2,803

Overall tax saving £1,333

2 Separate assessment of wife's income: Under this arrangement the overall tax position of you as a couple is *not* affected, but the application for this form of separate assessment results in the apportionment of the total tax payable between husband and wife, in proportion to your respective incomes. *The application must be made by either party to the marriage* within six months before 6th July falling in the year of assessment for which these provisions are to apply. There is the same time limit for revoking the election which must be done by the same spouse who originally made the election.

There is *no tax advantage in this form of separate assessment;* however, there are benefits in that the husband may no longer be required to make a return of his wife's income, since if she so wishes she may make her own return. Each person is liable to pay their own income tax and will receive individual assessments. On the other hand, if there is a repayment of tax due, that will also be sent to the appropriate individual.

● **11   What happens if our marriage comes to an end?**

For income tax purposes there are three ways in which a marriage can come to an end: *separation, divorce* or *death.* Technically the marriage is said to have ended when the parties 'cease living together' as man and wife. Separation can be formalised by a court order or by deed, but the term also covers the situation where the couple have separated in such circumstances that the separation is likely to be permanent, in which case a formal judicial separation order is not required.

If your marriage should come to an end, it will have the following effect on your income tax.

Husband: You will be allowed the married man's allowance for the whole of the tax year in which the marriage comes to an end (it is not apportioned as in the year of marriage), and from the following 6th April you will be taxed as a single man.

Wife: You will be treated as two separate people to and from the date the marriage comes to an end: before that date you will be given the wife's earned income allowance (if applicable) and your income will be deemed to be that of your husband. From the date of separation or death, you will be taxed as a single person, being given the single person's allowance; in case of death, see also question 26.

If the marriage has ended through separation or divorce it is quite likely there will be some form of maintenance payable by the husband in respect of his wife, their children, or both. It may be that the separation is amicable, in which case the husband may be making voluntary payments to maintain the family. If he, during the period of separation, is considered by the Revenue to be wholly maintaining his wife (taking into account any other income she receives) he will continue to be given the married man's personal allowance. If this is the case, the voluntary payments are not treated as the wife's income for tax purposes.

For payments made under a court order, it is important to distinguish between:

(1) income under a court order made in favour of the wife, which is her income;

(2) income under an order for the payments to be made to the wife (or any other person) for the maintenance of the children, which is also the recipient's income; and

(3) income under an order made in favour of the children direct, which is then their income.

If the payments are made direct to the children, each child will be granted the single person's allowance.

Payments made under a court order are defined as small maintenance payments if they do not exceed the following limits as regards payments made on or after 6th April 1986 (the limits for payments made before that date are shown in brackets):

for orders made under (1) or (3),
    £48 (£33) per week or £208 (£143) per month;
for orders made under (2),
    £25 (£18) per week or £108 (£78) per month.

(For this purpose a child must be under 21.) The payments are made gross with a tax allowance being given for the same amount to the payer. The payments are taxable in the hands of the recipient but although it is a source of unearned income all maintenance payments were specifically exempted from the investment income surcharge (see question 2).

There can also be payments made under a court order from which tax is deducted at source. This means that the husband deducts tax at the basic rate from the gross payments and pays only the net amount to his wife. The payments are treated as a charge on his income and can give relief at both the basic and higher rates of tax, as can be seen from the following example. The payments may also provide a repayment of income tax for the wife if her income is low.

Example

The marriage of Peter Out came to an end several years ago. He was ordered to pay his wife £3,000 each year, before deduction of tax. For 1986/87 his only income is earnings of £27,000.

If he was not paying maintenance, his liability to tax would be as follows.

	£
Income	27,000
less single person's allowance	2,335
Taxable income	£24,665
Charged as	
£17,200 at 29%	4,988
£3,000 at 40%	1,200
£4,465 at 45%	2,009
Total tax due	£8,197

The actual tax suffered is reduced as shown below, taking the £3,000 payment into consideration.

	£
Income	27,000
less maintenance payment	3,000
	24,000
less single person's allowance	2,335
Taxable income	£21,665
Charged as	
£17,200 at 29%	4,988
£3,000 at 40%	1,200
£1,465 at 45%	659
Net tax suffered	£6,847

This gives an overall saving of £1,350, which is made up of £870 retained out of the maintenance payments (not actually paid over to the Revenue) and £480 reduction in higher rate tax liability.

The maintenance payment has therefore had the effect of *increasing the amount charged at the basic rate* by £3,000 and *reducing the amount charged at higher rates* by £3,000. Obviously, the higher the rate of tax, the more relief is obtained. The wife will have received the net amount (£3,000 less tax of £870) and if this is her only income she can reclaim tax on her personal allowance, £2,335 at 29% = £677.

Note that if the husband has unearned income, maintenance payments are treated as applied against this before his earned income, so possibly reducing his liability to investment income surcharge when this is applied (see question 2).

It is also possible for a husband to make maintenance payments to his separated or divorced wife under a legal agreement made between them without the need for obtaining a formal court order. In this case the payment *must* be made under deduction of income tax as previously illustrated and there is no facility for making small payments gross. Note also that tax deductible payments *cannot* be made to minor children under a maintenance agreement and that a court order must always be obtained for such payments.

12   If I am a single parent family what can I claim?

There is an additional allowance which may be claimed if you are a person (either male or female) who is not entitled to the married man's allowance, but you have children in your care. The amount of the allowance is £1,320 for 1986/87 and £1,370 for 1987/88 (the difference between the lower and higher personal allowances); this is given *once only* irrespective of the number of children involved. If the allowance is being claimed following separation or divorce and both parents claim they are maintaining the children the allowance can be apportioned between them; if each parent is separately maintaining one or more of the children, each may be able to claim an allowance. The child must be resident with the claimant during the whole or part of the tax year; in addition, the child must also be a child of the claimant or if not, must be under 18 and maintained for the whole or part of the year at the claimant's expense. In any event the child must be born during the year of assessment or be under 16 at the commencement of the year of assessment; alternatively, the child may be over 16 and undergoing full-time instruction at a recognised educational establishment, or undergoing training by an employer, for not less than two years, for a trade, profession or vocation.

This allowance may also be claimed by a married man whose wife is totally incapacitated (physically or mentally) throughout the year.

● **13   How can I prepare for my retirement?**

During your working life you will pay national insurance contributions under a particular class (depending on whether you are an employee or self-employed), in the amounts laid down by the state. (See question 14 for more details regarding the various classes and amounts to be paid.) If you pay the full contributions for at least nine-tenths of your working life you will qualify for the full *basic retirement pension*. A woman entitled to a pension in her own right will normally receive it at the age of 60; a man at the age of 65. A married man will receive an additional amount for his wife but if she is entitled to pensions in respect of both her own and her husband's contributions, she may claim whichever is the higher pension.

In addition to paying national insurance contributions, if you are an employee you may also be paying into a pension scheme. There is the *state earnings-related pension scheme (SERPS)* operated by the Government, and since 1978 every employer has had to pay into the state scheme for all his employees unless he is running an *approved* private scheme in which case he can *contract out*.

If your employer has contracted out this will not affect your entitlement to the basic national insurance retirement pension or any other social security benefits.

Your employer may be running his scheme in-house or through a life assurance company, but irrespective of who is running the scheme, it *must be approved by the Inland Revenue Superannuation Funds Office* and by the *Occupational Pensions Board*. The benefits the scheme offers must be at least as good as those provided by the state scheme.

The state scheme offers a considerable improvement on the terms of pension schemes that were being run before 1978, with the benefits increasing in line with the increases in the RPI; however, there are still a number of disadvantages that the state scheme has compared with an occupational scheme that has been duly approved. There can be no flexibility on the age of retirement, nor can a tax-free lump sum be paid at retirement; there is generally no income tax relief for the individual's payments into the scheme, and earnings over £14,820 for 1986/87 and £15,340 for 1987/88 are unpensionable.

To a large extent these problems can be overcome by entering into an individual pension arrangement with an insurance company called a *top hat scheme*. If you have unpensioned salary (i.e. the amount over the above limits) an arrangement can be made for just the excess; it is also possible to build into such arrangements benefits missing from the state scheme, such as tax-free lump sums on retirement, death in service benefits and to a certain extent it can be inflation proofed.

If your employer pays the contributions they would not be classed as a benefit and you will not have to pay tax on that amount; on the other hand, you can obtain tax relief on your contributions provided they do not exceed 15% of your earnings.

Increasing concern has been expressed in recent years about the provision of pensions for individuals in employment, in that *occupational pension schemes* (i.e. those organised by employers) tend to provide the best benefit to long serving employees. Generally, they also work to the disadvantage of employees who change jobs, particularly those that move into a new job near (perhaps within five years of) retirement. Mobility of employment of this kind tends to be much more common now than a few years ago.

It is current Government policy to encourage the provision of pensions through the private sector and to reduce dependence on the state scheme. To this end, the Government issued a White Paper in December 1985, followed by an Inland Revenue consultative document 12 months later, proposing a number of fundamental changes in the pension scene. Legislation on this is intended to be included in the 1987 Finance Act so that the new arrangements can be implemented from April 1988.

1 The promotion of new *personal pension schemes* for employees which would have the following features:
(a) the tax privileges already available in conventional pension schemes, in particular deductibility up to certain limits of employees' contributions;
(b) the ability for the individual to take his scheme with him when he changes jobs;
(c) the facility to contract out of SERPS if he wishes.

2 The simplification of arrangements whereby an individual already in an occupational pension scheme can 'top up' his pension fund so as to maximise his benefits. This is done by paying *additional voluntary contributions* (AVC's).

3 The introduction of *simplified occupational pension schemes* to encourage more employers to set up schemes.

4 The encouragement of *industry-wide occupational schemes*.

5 Improved *transferability* between different types of scheme.

One feature of this change is likely to be the appearance of new 'pension providers', such as banks and building societies, as a result of the financial services reforms.

If you are self-employed you may wish to prepare for your retirement by taking out a *retirement annuity policy* (see question 45). *This also applies to people who are in non-pensionable employment* (i.e. those not in an approved scheme). There is a considerable range of self-employed pension schemes available, and the tax relief on the premiums must not be forgotten.

There are also avenues open to you such as *purchased life annuities*. This is where an individual invests some of his capital in an annuity; when he receives the annuity payments at a later date, part of the payment is treated as the return of his capital, and is not taxed; the remainder is taxed as unearned income. The split between capital and income will depend on the individual's age at the date of commencement of the annuity. There is *no tax relief on the cost of buying the annuity*. It is also possible for an individual aged over 65 to borrow on the security of his house, and provided that at least 90% of the loan is used to buy an annuity for himself (or him and his wife jointly) he can obtain tax relief on the loan interest paid (see question 18).

Another way of planning for your retirement is by careful investment of your capital in the years preceding that event, and there are various forms of investment to be considered (see question 20). Savings through life assurance can perhaps be bettered elsewhere, but life assurance should always be considered for protection purposes.

● **14   What national insurance contributions should I pay?**

Broadly, the amount of contributions payable depends on whether the individual is employed, self-employed or non-employed. There are numerous variations for people in particular circumstances and the Department of Health and Social Security publishes leaflets providing advice and guidance as to these. A brief summary of the general principles applicable to individuals in the three main categories mentioned is set out below. The contribution scales for 1986/87 and 1987/88 are given in Appendix 4.

Employees: Contributions are payable under Class 1 by both employees and employers on a sliding scale related to earnings. No contributions are payable where earnings are below £38 per week in 1986/87 or £39 per week in 1987/88. On earnings in excess of £295 per week in 1987/88 (£285 per week in 1986/87), no contributions are payable by employees although contributions continue to be payable by employers.

Where the employer has contracted out of the state scheme (see question 13), lower rates of contributions apply to earnings below £295 per week in 1987/88 (£285 in 1986/87).

An employee does not have to pay Class 1 contributions after age 65 (60 for a woman) provided he gives his employer a certificate of age exemption.

Self-employed: Contributions are payable in two ways by all self-employed individuals; *class 2* contributions at a flat rate and *Class 4* contributions at 6.3% on profits earned between certain limits. Half the amount of Class 4 contributions paid for a tax year are allowable as a deduction from the individual's total income tax for that year.

Where an individual is self-employed and also an employee, he is liable to pay Class 1 and 2 contributions (and possibly Class 4). Any excess will be refunded and it may be possible to arrange deferment of the Class 2 and 4 contributions until after the end of the year to avoid the need for a refund.

Non-employed: Voluntary flat rate contributions may be paid by an individual who wishes to improve his Class 1 or 2 contributions record to help in qualifying for a limited range of benefits.

15   If I am over 65 years of age, do I still pay tax? ●

Unfortunately, the UK tax system is not run in such a way as to automatically exempt you from tax when you reach the age of 65. If you are able to continue working after the normal retirement age, you will continue to pay tax on your income, and if you are receiving a pension, this too is taxable.

There is, however, an allowance which will be granted, if you are 65 or over in a year of assessment and your income falls within certain limits. In the case of a married couple it can be either the husband *or* the wife who is 65 or over to qualify for the relief.

This relief may be index-linked in the same way as the other main personal allowances. Currently the reliefs and income limit are as follows.

	1986/87	1987/88	
Age	65 or over	65-80	80 or over
Single person's age allowance	£2,850	£2,960	£3,070
Married man's age allowance	£4,505	£4,675	£4,845
Income limit (irrespective of whether claimant is single or married)	£9,400	£9,800	£9,800

It should be noted that age allowance is *not* available where the election for the separate taxation of the wife's earnings (see question 10) is in operation. In practice this is not as hard as it sounds: if the individual's earnings are sufficient to justify making the election, it is most unlikely that age allowance would be applicable in any case.

A word of warning here. Where the individual's total income exceeds the income limit shown above by a small amount the allowance is reduced by £2 for every £3 of excess income, until the amount comes down to the level of the normal single person's or married man's allowance. This can have a marked effect on the rate of tax applicable to the excess income, as the following example illustrates.

Example

A. Senior, a married man aged 70 has a total income of £9,400 in the tax year 1986/87. His tax liability on this is therefore:

	£
Total income	9,400
Age allowance	4,505
	£4,895
Income tax at 29%	£1,419

Now if his income for 1986/87 is £9,700, the calculation becomes:

	£	£
Total income		9,700
Age allowance	4,505	
Less abatement two-thirds of		
(9,700 − 9,400)	200.00	
		4,305
		£5,395
Income tax at 29%		£1,564

Mr Senior therefore has to pay extra tax of £145 on the additional income of £300, an effective rate of tax of 48.33%!

To avoid this situation, the taxpayer may like to seek ways of reducing his taxable income so as to restore the full age allowance and replace the shortfall by putting his money into investments which will produce capital gains rather than income. Commonly, as explained in Chapter 5, such gains would be covered by the annual exemption (£6,300 in 1986/87) and the indexation allowance; even if the gains are chargeable to capital gains tax (CGT), this will only be at 30%.

Other possible arrangements that can be used are:
1 Investing in National Savings Certificates (see question 20) and cashing these in at regular intervals to take advantage of the tax-free interest additions;
2 Investing in an investment bond (see question 20) and making annual withdrawals from this. Providing that these do not exceed 5% of the original cost per year, they will not normally be subject to income tax.

● 16   Are all social security benefits taxable?

There are approximately 40 different benefits which are payable by the Department of Health and Social Security *none of which is taxable;* these include maternity benefit and grants, invalidity pensions, student grants, family income supplement, child benefit, sickness benefit and mobility allowance.

The benefits listed below are all taxable as earned income.
Industrial death benefit
Invalid care allowance
Invalidity allowance when paid with retirement pension
Old person's pension
Retirement pension
War orphan's pension
Widowed mother's allowance
Widow's allowance
Widow's pension
Unemployment benefit
Certain privately-operated sickness scheme benefits

By concession, the *increase* in the amount of retirement pension and widows' benefits paid in July 1986 was exempt from tax for the tax year 1986/87. Following the next uprating of these benefits due in April 1987, the whole of the increased amount will be taxable in the normal way.

● 17   What income tax reliefs can I claim in respect of my home?

If you do not own your own home you cannot claim any allowance for the rent you pay. If you are buying your own home for which you have taken out a mortgage with a building society, you may wish to claim tax relief on the interest paid each year, thus reducing the amount of your taxable income.

Loans for the purchase, improvement or development of land, including buildings, are specifically allowable for tax purposes, provided certain conditions are met.

At the time the interest is paid the property must be the sole or main residence of the borrower, a dependent relative of the borrower (or his/her spouse) living there rent-free, or a separated spouse. The loan *must* be used for the purposes of purchasing or improving the house, and not just by way of borrowing capital using the house as security. The relief is limited to the first £30,000 of the loan. Also allowable for income tax purposes is a bridging loan taken out for the purchase of one residence with a view to the previous residence being sold; again the relief is limited to the first £30,000 of the loan.

It should be emphasised that in any case tax relief can only be claimed on the interest element of mortgage payments and not on capital repayments.

The next question you will no doubt ask is actually how to claim the tax relief due on the interest payments. Until 6th April 1983, payments were made gross and tax relief was given in PAYE coding or by assessment. After that date, for most people, payments are made under the MIRAS scheme. This stands for 'mortgage interest relief at source' and operates in the same way as tax relief for maintenance payments from which tax is deducted at source as described towards the end of question 11. This means that the tax relief is deducted from the gross payment due and only the net amount is paid to the building society or other lender.

If you are a basic rate taxpayer, once the net payment has been made there is no further tax relief due. However, if you are liable to pay tax at the higher rates you are entitled to further relief which will normally be given in your PAYE coding or in the assessment.

You cannot normally claim for the day-to-day running of your home but if you use part of your home as an office you may be able to claim a tax allowance in respect of lighting and heating etc. The Revenue is sometimes reluctant to allow such claims, taking the view that if an employer requires you to do 'paperwork' he will provide you with an office. However, claims are accepted if you can prove it is *necessary* to work at home, whether you are an employee or self-employed. *Beware,* however, of making a claim that you use part of your home *exclusively* for these purposes as you may find the exemptions from capital gains tax (CGT) on your own home is affected (see question 70).

18   What other loan interest can I claim?

The rules regarding relief for other loan interest are very strict and relief will not be granted unless the loan proceeds applied for meet the qualifying purpose within a reasonable length of time. Similarly, if the loan is used for some other purpose first, the relief will not be granted. There is no tax relief for overdraft interest or credit cards (or similar arrangements), unless it is incurred wholly and exclusively for the purposes of your business as a sole trader or partner and is charged directly in your business accounts.

Loan interest relief will be allowed if the proceeds of the loan are used for any of the following, all of which are *qualifying purposes:*

1 A loan in respect of property which is let at a commercial rent for at least 26 weeks of the year and when not being let, is available to be let or is undergoing repair. There may be some restrictions as to the relief available, but these do not apply when the property qualifies as furnished holiday accommodation (see question 24).

2 Provision is also made to cover the situation where the borrower is living in accommodation provided by the employer as one of the requirements of his job, but at the same time the employee is paying interest on a loan to buy a house which he is either using as a residence at the time or intends to so use within 12 months; this allows relief to be claimed for interest paid by the employee on a loan on a house bought in anticipation of moving out of his present 'job-related' living accommodation. A similar relief is available where the individual is self-employed and is required to live in 'job-related' accommodation. (Relief on maximum £30,000 loan only.)

3 A loan for purchase of plant or machinery for use in a trade if the borrower is a partner in the business, or for use in the borrower's office or employment. Relief is only granted in the tax year in which the loan is taken out and the following three years, and only if a claim for capital allowances on the plant and machinery has been granted.

4 A loan for purchase of ordinary shares in, or making a loan to a close company, subject to certain restrictions.

5 A loan for purchase of a share in, or making a loan to, a partnership. The lender must be a member of the partnership; where the money is lent to the partnership it must be used for the purposes of the partnership business.

6 A loan to make payment of capital transfer tax, estate duty or inheritance tax in respect of a deceased person. The relief is granted to the personal representatives, but for a period of one year only from the date of the loan.

7 A loan to purchase a life annuity by a borrower aged 65 or over. He must use his own home as security for the loan and at least 90% of the proceeds of the loan must be used to purchase the annuity (see question 13).

8 A loan to buy shares in an 'employee-controlled company'; this can arise where employees are given the opportunity to buy a con-

trolling interest in an unquoted company from its existing pro-
prietors (this again may be subject to some restrictions, depending
mainly on the percentage shareholding acquired by the individual).

19 Do I pay tax on my building society or bank interest? ●

Like most forms of interest received (other than bank interest,
which is looked at below), interest on deposit, savings, investment
and similar accounts with *building societies* is paid after deduction of
income tax. As a result of a special arrangement between the building
societies and the Inland Revenue, this tax is deducted at a special
rate, known as the *composite rate;* this is generally less than the
basic rate of income tax and is intended to reflect the average rate
of tax suffered by recipients of building society interest, recognising
that some of them do not pay tax at all. As a corollary to this, a
recipient who is not liable to income tax is *not* able to claim any
refund of this tax withheld by the building society. On the other
hand, a recipient who is liable to income tax is treated as having
received the interest as if tax *at the basic rate* had been deducted: if
he is only liable to tax at the basic rate, no further tax is payable; if
he is liable to tax at higher rates (including the 15% investment
income surcharge up to 1983/84, see question 2), the additional tax
will be assessed on him directly.

Previously *bank* interest was *not* taxed before receipt and it was
therefore wholly taxable in the recipient's hands. The normal basis
of assessment was on the 'preceding year', i.e. whatever was credited
to your bank account in one tax year was taxed in the following tax
year. There were special rules for the interest credited during the
opening and closing years of a bank account when the interest could
be taxed in the same year that it was credited to the account.

This basis applied for interest credited up to 5th April 1985. After
that date, bank interest is treated in the same way as building society
interest, as described above, with the banks subject to the same
composite rate tax arrangement. Recipients of such interest are
regarded as receiving interest less tax at the basic rate but will not be
able to claim back any refund of that tax; they will still be liable to
further tax at the higher rates if this is applicable (see question 2).

In the final tax year 1984/85 in which the old arrangement applied,
tax was charged on the *actual* interest credited in that year and the
'preceding year' basis mentioned above did not apply.

An individual who is *not ordinarily resident* in this country with a deposit account at a UK branch may apply to his bank to continue to have the interest credited to him gross as before. From 6th April 1986, the facility is also available for interest paid to such an individual by a building society.

Bodies such as charities which are exempt from tax may also arrange to have bank and (with effect from 6th April 1986) building society interest paid to them gross.

Interest on certain deposits with *local authorities* continued to be paid gross until 5th April 1986, after which the composite rate tax system applied to them also.

It should also be noted that this arrangement does *not* apply to a bank deposit account held outside the UK, for instance at the Jersey branch of a UK bank, by an individual who is resident in this country. Interest on such an account will continue to be paid gross and assessed to income tax on the recipient as described above.

Interest credited to the National Savings Bank *ordinary* account is exempt up to £70 a year for an individual. If you are married, each spouse will be entitled to the £70 exemption but any excess of one spouse's exemption *cannot* be given to the other. Any interest in excess of £70 is still paid gross but liable to tax in the usual way. Note, the exemption *does not* apply to the National Savings Bank *investment* account.

● 20   Where should I invest my capital?

This is a topic which could be the subject matter of a book in its own right. There is no answer because matters such as the availability of your capital (i.e. the need to have quick access to capital), provision for your dependents, how much you want to invest and your own personal tax position must be taken into consideration. It is therefore not possible to list different forms of investment and to advise on which ones to use without knowing about your overall financial position–this is something for you to discuss with your professional advisers. What follows therefore are a few *general* words of advice.

There are certain types of investment on which you *do not* pay tax; these include the *National Savings Bank* ordinary account (see question 19) where up to £70 interest can be credited to your account without tax being payable. There are also *National Savings Certificates,* on which interest, bonuses and any other sums are exempt from all forms of tax; there is a limit to the number of these you may hold. There is also a special index-linked issue (previously known as 'granny bonds'). You may wish to invest in *Premium Bonds*–if you do so, remember there is no interest on the amount invested but if you should win, your winnings are not taxable.

You may also invest in the *National Savings Yearly Plan*. This allows you to subscribe a regular amount from £20 to £200 per month to buy a *Yearly Plan Savings Certificate* at the end of the year. These certificates earn a guaranteed rate of interest (tax free) which increases the longer the certificates are held.

Many people invest their capital in *building societies*–indeed very often this is a necessity if you are hoping to obtain a mortgage–and the interest you receive is net of tax. A point to note arises here: if you are not liable to pay tax at all, investing your money in a building society or in a bank deposit account in the UK is *not* a good idea, as you are deemed to have paid tax on the interest but this cannot be reclaimed, as explained in question 19.

The rate of interest on ordinary share accounts is quite reasonable but if you do not require immediate access to your capital a *Save As You Earn (SAYE) Scheme* through a building society is always a good investment. Such an investment is one of the best ways to earn a high rate of interest, but it is a longer term commitment to saving, as you will be required to pay a fixed sum every month for a period of up to five years. Beware of stopping the payments early as penalties can be incurred. A similar scheme operated by the Department of National Savings was withdrawn in May 1984.

Whatever the amount of capital you wish to invest you will obviously require a certain amount that is realisable to provide cash in an emergency but you may wish to consider investing in *Government gilt-edged stocks*. The income you receive from these investments is taxed at source (at the basic rate of tax) and after 2nd July 1986 there is no liability to capital gains tax (previously the exemptions from that tax only applied if the stock was held for more than 12 months: see question 66).

Certain issues of gilt-edged stocks are inflation linked, providing a measure of tax-free capital appreciations which could be attractive to higher rate tax payers.

Another worthwhile form of investment is the *single premium investment bond*. A capital sum is invested with an insurance company; the income is taxable but you are allowed to withdraw each year up to 5% of the initial value invested and these withdrawals are not immediately taxed. They are taken into account in the year the bond is surrendered, so that higher rate tax may be payable in this final year. It is possible, however, to reduce this liability with careful planning, by making sure that the year of encashment is one when other income is low.

If you are already a higher-rate tax payer you should be seeking to minimise your tax liability, possibly by aiming for capital growth. This may result in you having to withdraw from time to time capital to supplement your income, unless you also have other forms of investment.

If you are considering investing directly on the stock market, for many people unit trusts represent the most sensible and effective way of doing so. The clearing banks and Trustee Savings Bank offer a wide range of savings schemes which could also be considered.

With effect from 1st January 1987, a new form of tax efficient investment, known as the *Personal Equity Plan* (PEP), was introduced as an incentive to encourage savings through the purchase of quoted shares. This allows an individual to invest up to £2,400 a year (which may be in regular monthly amounts or in a lump sum) through an authorised plan manager, such as a bank or stockbroker, in a separate fund on his behalf. Provided that a number of conditions are satisfied, the most important of which is that the investment must remain in the plan for at least a full calendar year, then interest and dividends on the plan investments that are reinvested in the plan are free of income tax. A similar exemption from CGT applies to reinvested capital gains. This means that money invested in a plan during 1987 must stay there throughout 1988 and cannot be withdrawn until 1989 at the earliest in order to take advantage of the exemptions.

It should be noted that the plan manager will levy certain charges for his services, which will reduce the value of the income tax exemption. So far as the CGT exemption is concerned, an investor is entitled to an annual exemption in any case (£6,600 in 1987/88, see question 65). Thus the PEP's exemption may not be of any value unless the investor expects to use up his annual exemption in any case.

With an uncertain future with regard to inflation, it is wise to have a *flexible investment policy* rather than allow yourself to become too restricted. It might well be prudent, therefore, even if your aim is for a higher income, to invest some of your funds in investments producing lower income than perhaps could be obtained otherwise, in order to achieve *flexibility,* the *security* of your capital, and the prospects of *capital growth*–all to try and beat inflation.

21 Can a deed of covenant save me tax? ●

Deeds of covenant do not provide spectacular tax savings, but they are nevertheless useful weapons for you to have. They can be very simple to create and easy to operate. They do not involve a commitment for too long a period and they can provide useful savings in a variety of situations.

A deed of covenant is the 'gratuitous transfer' by one person (the 'covenantor') of some part of his income to another person (the 'beneficiary'). Below are two of the main provisions which limit the use of deeds of covenant in tax planning:

1 If the income is given for a period not exceeding six years 'it is not recognised for tax purposes'–hence the familiar seven-year covenant.

2 The transfer of income by a parent to a child under 18 and unmarried has no effect for tax purposes as this income is still deemed to be that of the parent. The covenant can still be effective, however, if it is made by a grandparent or other relative.

The 'seven-year' rule calls for a little care–the period covered by the deed of covenant must be able to *exceed* six years to qualify for tax purposes–it is no good making the payment 'for six years' as this clearly cannot exceed the limit. Thus, the deed of covenant must either be of a *definite duration exceeding six years* or of *an indefinite duration* which is *capable of exceeding six years,* examples of this are the lifetime of the covenantor or the beneficiary or, if the covenant is in respect of a child, until the beneficiary *ceases in full-time education.* At first glance, if the beneficiary is taking only a three year course this would not seem to qualify, but if the beneficiary was to fail exams it may be that his educational time is extended–in other words, the period is *capable* of exceeding six years.

On the other hand, if the duration of the covenant was for the lifetime of the covenantor and he (unfortunately) died after four years, the 'duration' test is still fulfilled. At the time the covenant was made, its duration was for an indeterminate period (i.e. the lifetime of the covenantor) *capable* of exceeding six years.

Deeds of covenant in respect of children over 18 attending university are popular, which is why the above illustration concerning the duration of the covenant has been used. The abolition of tax allowances for children has greatly increased the usefulness of deeds of covenant, particularly where the child is a student at university and the parent is expected, under the grant regulations, to make a contribution to the student's maintenance.

Parents are not asked to make a contribution if their income is insufficient, so if you are asked to contribute, your income must be high enough to warrant you paying at least the basic rate tax. *For the covenant to be effective you must be paying tax on at least the same amount of your income, as the amount of the covenant.* In other words, tax on the amount you are to pay has already been deducted from you (albeit on your other income). If you make a covenant in respect of your child (possibly equal to the amount of the parental contribution for the first year) *you will only have to pay the net amount* to your son or daughter: in other words, tax is deducted before the student receives it and you have saved the tax on the payment. It is advisable to keep the amount of the covenant to within the single personal allowance (which the child is entitled to) as *he can then reclaim all the tax that was deducted,* by making a claim to the Inland Revenue. In effect he will then have received the covenanted payment gross.

Example

Ivor Sunn's eldest boy Jack is at university and his father is required to contribute £1,650 per annum towards his maintenance. He therefore enters into a deed of covenant for an annual amount which after deduction of income tax at the basic rate for the time being will leave £1,650, for a period of seven years, the lifetime of the covenantor or beneficiary or the period during which the beneficiary is undergoing full-time education or training. Jack has no other taxable income in the year 1987/88.

The net cost to the father is the amount he actually pays, i.e. £1,650 per year. Jack is treated as receiving income of £2,260 gross less income tax at 27% i.e. £610; because his taxable income is less than the single personal allowance for the year (£2,425) he is not liable to income tax in 1987/88 and can therefore reclaim the £610 treated as deducted, from the Inland Revenue, giving him a total actual income of £2,260.

In order to substantiate the claim it is essential that the amount provided in the deed of covenant is actually paid over to the beneficiary.

A deed of covenant is a formal legal document and must be properly drawn up to have the required effect. Most charities (see question 22) use standard forms which have been approved by the Inland Revenue for this purpose; in other cases it is *essential* to obtain proper advice on the drafting of a deed of covenant to ensure that it works. The Inland Revenue has introduced a pack (IR59) specially tailored to the needs of students; this includes a standard form of deed and repayment claim form, and some helpful information on the procedure to be followed.

22   How can I give money to charity in a tax efficient way?   ●

A similar arrangement to that described in question 21 applies to covenanted payments to *charities*. As charities are exempt from tax they are able to recover from the Inland Revenue the income tax treated as deducted from the payments made by the donor at no extra cost to the latter, thus providing a substantial boost to their own revenue.

There are two points applying to covenanted payments to charities which are of particular importance:
1 A deed of covenant to a charity need only run for a period 'capable of exceeding *three* years' instead of six, as the general rule requires; this it is hoped will encourage people to commit themselves for four years when they might have been reluctant to go on for seven years.
2 A covenantor is able to obtain relief for higher rate tax purposes for such payments made to charities. It should be emphasised that the charity can still only recover the basic rate element of tax, but the real cost to the donor will be reduced by the further tax relief he can claim if he is paying income tax at more than the basic rate.

Example (using 1987/88 tax rates)

		£
Charitable covenant		73 net p.a.
(taxpayer paying top rate of 60%)		
Income tax, recoverable by charity		27
		£100
Gross equivalent		100
Income tax relief due		
to covenantor by deemed		
deduction at 27%	27	
relief at (60–27)%	33	60
Net cost to donor		£40

In his Budget speech on 18th March 1986 the Chancellor of the Exchequer announced a new *payroll deduction scheme,* to operate from April 1987, whereby employers will be able to arrange for their employees to make deductions from their wages and salaries and for these deductions to be paid over to specified charities. These deductions will qualify for tax relief up to £120 a year.

● **23   Can I set aside money towards my taxes?**

It is possible to set money aside to pay your taxes by way of *certificates of tax deposit.* Some people prefer this method of payment of tax to having to withdraw money from another source to pay their tax bills. The deposits are made with the Collector of Taxes for the subsequent payment of tax generally (except for PAYE and tax deducted from subcontractors in the construction industry). The minimum initial deposit is £2,000 with minimum additions of £500. Interest is payable gross, but is taxable, and this will accrue for a maximum of six years from the date of deposit to the date the tax is due to be paid. If a deposit is withdrawn for cash at any time, a reduced rate of interest will apply.

● **24   I have other sources of income which are not taxed at source: how are they taxed?**

Two of the most common of the other types of income you may receive which are not taxed at source are income from furnished lettings and property. These are dealt with as follows.

Furnished lettings: An assessment is made on the profits arising in the year, which is rent received less rent paid, repairs, rates, commission and any other expenses relating to the letting. There are also allowances to be claimed for wear and tear of the furniture.

The profits from lettings of *holiday accommodation* may be treated as earned income with effect from 6th April 1982, provided that certain tests are met. The most important of these are:

(a) The property is available for letting to the general public as furnished residential accommodation for at least 140 days in the tax year.

(b) It is actually so let for at least 70 days.

(c) During a period of at least seven months (which need not be continuous but which does include the actual periods of letting in (b)), each occupancy does not normally exceed 31 days.

Income from property: Tax is charged on rents received from property including rents from leases of land and buildings, ground rents, feu duties, etc. The assessments are made on the basis of receipts arising in the year of assessment, less allowable deductions such as repairs, rates, electricity, etc., insurance premiums, valuation fees, costs of rent collection.

For both these types of income–make sure you claim all the expenses to keep the taxable amount to a minimum.

25 If I have income subject to overseas taxation can I get any relief in the UK?

The UK tax system is such that it taxes income wherever it arises if the person entitled to receive it is resident here. If you are entitled to receive income from overseas, due to the fact that other countries have similar wide powers of taxation, it is inevitable that some income will be taxed twice. Although it may be impossible to avoid this altogether, in many cases where income suffers tax in two countries it is possible to claim *double taxation relief.*

There are double taxation treaties between the UK and some 90 other countries and in general, either a particular source of income is exempt from tax in one of the countries involved, or the relief for foreign direct taxation is given as a credit against the corresponding UK tax.

This is a complex area and special consideration needs to be given to each situation.

26 What happens when I die?

When you die, if there is outstanding income tax to pay this liability will have to be met by your personal representatives. The implications for CGT and inheritance tax (IHT) are dealt with elsewhere.

If you are married the tax position depends on which spouse dies first. If the wife dies first, the husband will still be entitled to claim the married man's personal allowance for the whole of the tax year, and from the start of the next tax year he will be taxed as a single person. It is possible for the husband (or his executors) to disclaim responsibility for the wife's share of tax outstanding at her death, provided due notice is given to the Inland Revenue, normally within two months of the grant of probate.

If it is the husband who dies first, the wife's income from the beginning of the tax year to the date of his death is included in his final assessment to tax. She is then treated as a single person for the remainder of that tax year and subsequent years, being given the lower personal allowance (see question 5) against her income which presumably will include a widow's pension. In addition, a *widow's bereavement allowance* may also be claimed by the widow for the year in which her husband dies. The relief is available against her income following his death and is equivalent to the difference between the single and married man's personal allowance (i.e. for 1986/87, £1,320; 1987/88, £1,370). The allowance may be claimed if the husband was 'entitled' to the married person's allowance, even if the allowance had actually been foregone due to a wife's earnings election being in force. The allowance is also available in the tax year following that in which the husband died, provided that the widow has not remarried before the beginning of that later tax year.

2 YOU HAVE EARNED IT

TAXATION OF THE EMPLOYEE

27   What is included in my earnings for income tax purposes and ●
how are they taxed under the PAYE system?

Earnings from an office or employment come under many different names such as salaries, wages, fees, overtime, bonuses, commission, tips and gratuities, etc. *In general, anything which you receive as a reward for your services is taxable,* and the words 'emoluments' and 'remuneration' are often used to cover all receipts of this nature.

Having decided what is taxable, the next problem is how is it taxed? As an employee, you are probably only too well aware of the tax that is deducted from the pay you receive each week or month under the *Pay As You Earn* (PAYE) scheme.

The PAYE system was introduced in 1943 to replace other less successful methods of taxing the earnings of employees. It was not introduced as a new method of assessment; it was, and still is, merely a *scheme for the collection of tax.* Its aim is to deduct tax from each payment of remuneration, the deduction rising and falling as the pay rises and falls, so that at the end of the income tax year, the tax deducted during the year is sufficient having regard to the employee's personal circumstances and no further action is necessary.

The backbone of the system is the *cumulative* principle under which, as the tax year progresses, running (cumulative) totals are kept of the amounts of remuneration received from the beginning of the tax year and of the tax deducted. Each time your employer pays remuneration he will deduct (or refund) an amount of tax which will keep the total figure deducted correct. He can tell what this figure should be from tax tables which are supplied by the Inland Revenue. The process continues up to week 52 or month 12, when a new income tax year starts, and you commence at week 1 or month 1 again. Special procedures apply where there are 53 pay days in the year!

You already know that the amount of tax payable is governed by your personal circumstances and there are certain reliefs and allowances you may claim. If the employer is to deduct the right amount of tax it would seem that he too must have knowledge of your personal circumstances but the Revenue are bound not to reveal to anyone the private information given to them. The difficulty is resolved by the use of *codings,* with a number and a letter from which the employer can only tell certain things (i.e. in most cases he can tell if you are a single or married man, but if you do not wish him to know this, it can be prevented). The allowances to which you are entitled are added together and the coding applicable to this is notified to the employer–*the higher the coding, the lower the tax.* Your employer will only be informed of the final coding but you will be sent a notice showing your allowances and how the resulting coding is arrived at; if you disagree with it you may appeal against it. Similarly, if your personal circumstances change during the year the Revenue should be notified and your coding will be amended. Because of the cumulative principle mentioned above, a change of coding has retrospective effect to the previous 6th April. If it is increased, the tax overdeducted in previous weeks or months is refunded by your employer. If it is decreased, a special basis called week 1 or month 1 is used, otherwise the tax underdeducted in the previous weeks would be deductible in one sum, and this could cause hardship. In effect, in this situation the cumulative principle is abandoned for that year, and the employer deducts tax on each pay day without reference to previous pay. (See question 28 for what happens to the tax underdeducted for the earlier part of the year.)

The previous paragraphs may give the impression that employees stay with one employer all the time but, of course, people change their jobs, school leavers start work for the first time, elderly people retire and in fact there is a constant movement. To cater for this within the PAYE system, when you leave one employer he will give you a form known as a P45 which shows your coding, pay and tax to date. This form must be given to your new employer to enable him to continue the cumulative deductions of tax. If you lose your P45, or for some other reason are starting work without it, your employer will use a special coding so that your tax does not fall too far into arrears, and will inform the Revenue so that they may start the procedure for issuing the correct coding.

It should be noted that unemployment benefit is taxable as earned income (see question 16). The actual benefit payments are made without deduction of tax to benefit claimants, but these are then taken into account in determining whether any part of the tax deducted under PAYE prior to the period of unemployment is to be refunded. Any refund is made only when the individual starts work again or at the end of the tax year, whichever is the sooner.

28   If I pay tax under PAYE will I also be assessed at the end of each year? If so, how will I be assessed?

It has already been explained that the PAYE system is not a method of assessment but simply a way of collecting the tax. The next point to consider is how much of the earnings are assessed for a particular year. *The proper basis of assessment is to assess the amount actually earned in the year of assessment.* Most employees receive at the end of each week or month the amount of money they have actually earned during that period. If at the end of the tax year they are therefore assessed on what they have earned, this is the same figure as the amount they have received and tax has already been deducted. The employer sends to the Revenue details of each person's pay and tax deducted, on what is called a *deduction working sheet*–the details are checked and if the tax deducted is correct, no further action is normally required.

If you ask for an assessment because you think you have paid the wrong amount of tax the Revenue will do as you ask, but the Revenue also has the right to make an assessment where it considers it is necessary. This includes situations where there is tax owing for an earlier year, or where an allowance has been given incorrectly. Any refund of tax due to you resulting from the assessment is repaid to you, but if there is an underpayment of tax this will be collected from you.

This is normally achieved by restricting your coding allowances for the following year, although there are occasions when you will be asked to make payment of the tax to the Collector of Taxes. (You may voluntarily pay the tax to the Collector if you prefer this method of payment rather than having your coding allowances restricted.) Also collected through a later coding adjustment are underpayments arising because an allowance was removed from the coding part way through a year and there is tax to pay for the period before the coding was amended. If, in any of these instances, to collect the tax in one year would cause hardship this may be spread over a period of up to three years. No action is taken to collect small amounts and a lenient view is normally taken of pensioners.

Cases like these do not normally present any real problem but in situations where there are *substantial fluctuations in remuneration* (e.g. fees, bonuses, commission, etc.), the basis of assessment is more complicated as the payment of the remuneration is often made in a different tax year to when it was actually earned. *The assessment must exclude any payments made during the year which relate to a previous year, and include payments relating to the year in question but which will not be paid until after the end of the tax year.* This is called the 'earnings' basis of assessment and the business accounts of the employer must be consulted to see what commissions etc. have been voted during the tax year so that the assessment is correct, although payment may not be made to the individual until a later date. Any payments which relate to more than one tax year are apportioned to arrive at the actual amount *earned* in each year.

As part of the information necessary to raise an assessment is taken from the employer's business accounts, there may be some delay before the details are available and the assessment is therefore also delayed. To prevent this delay there is an alternative basis of assessment, which, although it has no legal foundation, may nevertheless be acceptable both to the Inland Revenue and yourself. On this basis the assessment is made on the figure of remuneration shown in the employer's accounts for the accounting year that ends in the year of assessment (this is known as the 'accounts year' basis of assessment). This avoids the necessity of apportioning the income for the accounting year over two income tax years. The method of strict apportionment is always used when the income first arises and ceases. The Revenue will not use the 'accounts year' basis unless they have your written agreement. (If you have a problem as to how your remuneration should be assessed, you should seek professional advice.)

Although the figure of remuneration shown in an employer's records at the end of the tax year is not always used in an assessment, the figure of tax deducted is always used. It may well be that because of this an underpayment of tax is thrown up, but in most cases this will be carried forward to the later year when the payment is made of remuneration that has already been assessed, and the tax paid at the time will cover the underpayment. The Revenue will not normally seek to collect tax on remuneration which you have not yet received.

29 How much can I receive tax free if I cease my employment?

First of all, one very important point must be made–if you have a contract of employment which provides for a termination payment, such a sum is taxable in full. Apart from this, termination payments may be made tax free up to £25,000; on the next £25,000, the tax payable is reduced by a half, and on the £25,000 above that by a quarter. Any excess over £75,000 is taxable in full.

A payment in lieu of notice cannot be taxed at the time that it is made, as it is not regarded as remuneration (even if it is made under a clause in the contract of employment, because this option is in any case open to an employer under the employment legislation). However, it must be included with any other termination payments for the purpose of applying the reliefs maintained in the previous paragraph.

It is important that termination payments are correctly identified and that references to them in correspondence, minutes of board meetings, etc. are worded in a way that does not suggest that they are payments for past or future services as then they could be charged to tax as income from that employment.

To obtain the maximum benefit for this relief it is helpful to keep other income as low as possible in the year in which the payment is taxable, so if a new employment is to be taken up immediately, termination should be as near to the end of the tax year as possible.

Statutory redundancy payments are exempt from tax but may still need be taken into account in these calculations.

A rather curious situation came to light in June 1986. The law relating to termination payments was amended in 1982, as set out in the preceding paragraph. But owing to a drafting error that slice of the termination payment on which tax was to be reduced by a half was fixed at £50,000, not £25,000 as intended and indeed as everybody (Inland Revenue, professional advisers and taxpayers) believed. When this error was discovered, the law was hurriedly corrected with effect from 4th June 1986 so as to ensure that only £25,000 ranked for relief in this way.

However, the correction was not made retrospective, so that it is possible if an individual was entitled to a termination payment of more than £50,000 in the period 6th April 1982 to 3rd June 1986, both dates inclusive, he may now be entitled to make a supplementary claim for relief and to receive a repayment of tax. This could amount to as much as £7,500 (i.e. half of £25,000 at 60%) plus repayment supplement. Any such supplementary claim must be made within six years of the end of the tax year in which the termination of employment took place. (Note, it is the date of *termination* that is critical for this purpose *not* the date of payment.)

● 30 Are perks taxable?

Most employees like a job that has perks and many employers nowadays run some form of incentive scheme or give their employees a benefit of some description. Unfortunately, the majority of these *fringe benefits,* as they are called, are taxable, although in some cases this depends on whether you are a higher paid employee (defined as one whose earnings are at a rate of £8,500 a year or more) or a director (in which case the level of your remuneration is irrelevant). It should be noted that 'remuneration' is specially defined for the purposes of this £8,500 threshold, so as to include the value of benefits and of expenses reimbursed before any deductions are allowed. Because of the method of taxing fringe benefits, it is nearly always to your advantage to be given an item as a benefit instead of having to buy the same item out of your own net income, which has already suffered tax.

It is not possible to list in this book all the possible benefits your employer may consider, but the following table mentions some of the more popular choices.

The special rules relating to company cars (still far and away the most popular perk) are dealt with in question 31.

As has already been stated, this is only a brief outline of the taxation of some of the fringe benefits: if you wish to known more about these matters you should seek professional advice.

Benefit	Directors and employees earning over £8,500 per annum	Employees earning less than £8,500 per annum
Holidays	Taxable in full unless combined with a business trip when the 'holiday element' may still be taxable	Not taxable providing employer pays direct and does not reimburse employee
Season tickets	Taxable	Taxable
Suggestion scheme payments	Not taxable provided it is within specified limits and not a term of contract	As aside
Prize incentive schemes	Taxable	Taxable
Examination prizes	Not taxable (as for suggestion schemes)	As aside
Canteen facilities	Not taxable provided available in one form or another to *all* staff	Not taxable
Luncheon vouchers	Not taxable provided not in excess of 15p per day	As aside
Credit cards	Taxable	Taxable
Medical insurance	Taxable on cost to employer. *Not* taxable if insurance against cost of treatment abroad where occasioned while employee performing duties outside UK	Not taxable

Benefit	Directors and employees earning over £8,500 per annum	Employees earning less than £8,500 per annum
Welfare, sports and social facilities	Not taxable	Not taxable
Use of company-owned assets by employees, e.g. furniture, housing	Taxable on 'annual value' when use begins; generally 20% of cost of asset, special rules for houses	Not taxable
Transfer of company-owned assets other than cars to employees	Taxable on market value when first used by employee less benefit already charged to him (as above) or on market value at time of transfer, if greater	Taxable on market value at time of transfer
Transfer of company car to employee	Taxable on market value at time of transfer	Taxable on market value at time of transfer
Scholarships awarded to employees' children	Taxable	Not taxable
Nursery facilities	Up to 5th April 1985 *by concession* not taxable. Taxable from 6th April 1985	Not taxable

● **31   What is my tax position if I have a company car, or use my own car for business purposes?**

If you are provided with a company car and you use it for your own private purposes, you are obviously deriving a benefit from this, simply due to the fact that you are using a car that does not belong to you for your own private use. On the other hand, if you are using your own car for business purposes this must benefit your employer and if he does not reimburse the expenses you incur, you would be out of pocket. This is, in simple terms, the way you and your car are considered for tax purposes.

If you are a director or a higher paid employee (as defined, see question 30) and you have a company car, you are taxed on what the Revenue considers is the benefit you receive from using the car for your own use. This is often referred to as the 'table benefit' because the benefit is decided according to the age, cost and cylinder capacity of the car, set out in tables included in the legislation. For the current year, if your business mileage exceeds 18,000 the benefit is *reduced to one half.* On the other hand, if your business mileage is less than 2,500 miles a year this is classed as insubstantial and the benefit is one and a half times the normal figure; this increase also applies to a second car provided by the employer. If you use your own car for business purposes you may claim a tax allowance as if you are self-employed (see question 44) but when the allowance has been computed any amount received from your employer as reimbursement is deducted.

Petrol provided by an employer for the private use of a director or higher paid employee (as defined, see question 30) is also taxed according to tables similar to those referred to in the previous paragraph. See also question 100 regarding the VAT treatment of petrol provided for private use with effect from 6th April 1987 onwards.

The tables of the car and car petrol benefits for 1986/87 and 1987/88 are shown in Appendix 3.

Where the employee makes a contribution to the employer towards the cost of providing the car, the corresponding 'car' benefit is reduced by that amount. However, no reduction is made to the 'car petrol' benefit for any contribution towards the cost of petrol unless the employee is required to reimburse that amount provided for private use *and* does so, *or* if petrol is made available only for business use; in that case, the car petrol benefit is reduced to nil. No reduction is made where the employee is required to reimburse a proportion of the petrol cost or if he makes a voluntary contribution towards the cost. It follows that where an employee does make some contribution towards his employer's costs, this should, as far as possible, be attributed to the use of the car, thus reducing the taxable benefit, rather than the provision of petrol, with no such reduction.

Where an employee has a relatively low private mileage, it may be to his advantage to forego the car petrol benefit altogether and pay for his own private petrol.

In any event *no allowance* is given for *travelling from home to work* as this is not classed as business mileage. The rule is that such expenses must be incurred *wholly and exclusively* in 'the performance of the duties of the employment' to be allowable and this does not generally cover travelling expenses *to* that place of employment, although this rule may be modified where the employee is required to use his home as his base and only occasionally visit his office.

● **32   How can I check that my PAYE coding is correct?**

As mentioned in question 27, a notice should be sent to each employee showing what allowances he is entitled to (or considered by the Revenue to be entitled to), and how his PAYE coding is arrived at. In practice, a notice of coding is not necessarily issued each year and it may therefore be helpful if an employee carries out his own check against the Revenue's coding as operated by his employer. The employee will need to follow this procedure.

1 Add up the allowances (for most people this will be either the single person's or married man's allowance, see questions 5 and 6);

2 Deduct from 1 the amounts of any benefits in kind assessable on him (see questions 30 and 31);

3 Also deduct any restriction for underpaid PAYE for earlier years (see question 28);

4 Divide the result by ten.

This result, rounded up, should be the individual's coding.

Note, no adjustment is made for mortgage interest paid under MIRAS (see question 17), unless the individual is a higher rate taxpayer, nor is there an adjustment for any life assurance premiums paid (see question 7), as the relief due will normally be given by deduction at source.

A typical example of this for 1987/88 might be as shown in the following table.

	£	£
Married man's allowance		3,795
Deduct: car benefit for 2,200cc car less than four years old (business miles 2,500 plus)	1,100	
car petrol benefit	900	
		2,000
		1,795
Deduct restriction for £58 tax underpaid from 1984/85 (taxpayer's rate assumed to be 40%)		145
		£1,650
Divide by 10		£165

If the employee's coding differs from this he should seek an explanation from the Revenue.

Where the individual has more than one employer, his allowances and deductions are normally given against one employment only and a coding fixed accordingly. Special codings are then given for his other employments so that these are taxed at a fixed rate, estimated to recover more or less the right amount of tax in total over the tax year.

Where there is a change in the overall level of allowances, for example an increase in the single person's or married man's allowances (see questions 5 and 6), the Inland Revenue will advise employers on a block basis as to how much their employees' codings should be changed by. Therefore, an individual employee need not take any action. There is usually some time lag in bringing the new codings into operation; thus for 1987/88, although the new personal allowances were announced on 17th March 1987, they will not actually take effect until the first pay day after 17th May. As described in question 27, because of the cumulative principle the changes will then be retrospective to the beginning of the tax year, 6th April 1987.

● **33 I have always lived in this country but part of my work is now done abroad: can I claim any tax relief?**

You are now entering into the complicated areas of domicile and residence and it is important for you to have a basic understanding of these terms before the reliefs available for work done abroad are explained. However, what follows in this section is simplified and some matters are mentioned only briefly.

Generally, your *domicile* is the country you think of as your natural homeland, which is normally that of your origin at birth. It is possible to change your domicile to one of your choice, but only if you sever all connections with the country of your origin and produce evidence of your intention to settle permanently in the other country.

Once it is known in what country you are domiciled, your *residence status* has to be decided for a tax year as this can decide how much of your earnings are taxed for that year, as you will see later. There are three terms involved here–resident, ordinarily resident and not resident. *Resident* and *not resident* are factual terms meaning, as you would expect, that you are either living in this country at the time or you are not. The term *ordinarily resident* refers to someone who normally lives in this country, although he may be abroad at the present time. A wife's residence status is independent of that of her husband; if their status should differ for a tax year, husband and wife are treated as separate individuals unless it is to their disadvantage.

The following reliefs apply to someone who is *domiciled, resident and ordinarily resident* in the UK, and whose *employer* is also *resident* in this country.

Where the duties of an employment are performed wholly or partly outside the UK and the time spent abroad is at least 365 days, there is no UK tax on these earnings; this is referred to as the '100% deduction'. There are provisions relaxing the 365 day requirement when time spent in this country does not exceed 62 consecutive days or one-sixth of the time elapsed since the first day of absence (this last rule can operate harshly towards the beginning of a lengthy absence period). The deduction is only available against the earnings in respect of work performed abroad (i.e. normally earnings in respect of work done in this country are fully taxable).

Up to 5th April 1985, a more limited form of relief was available for *short absences* abroad, meaning periods of 30 days or more in any tax year but not sufficient to qualify for the 100% deduction described above. The relief was calculated by taking the proportion of the remuneration attributable to work done abroad, usually calculated on a strict time basis by reference to the number of days of absence from the UK as a fraction of 365. Up to 1983/84, the relief given was 25% of this proportion of the remuneration; for 1984/85, the relief given was at 12.5%, and for subsequent years has been withdrawn altogether.

Travelling expenses to and from an overseas employment are not taxable where these are met by the employer; also tax free are board and lodging and expenses of travelling between different overseas employments. Costs of travel for wife and children may also be included under certain conditions.

If you are leaving the country to work abroad you are required to complete a questionnaire for the Revenue so that a ruling can be made as to your residence status. In the situations looked at so far the employer is resident in the UK so he will operate PAYE in the usual way (see question 27). Where it is clear that the 100% deduction will apply, a special coding is issued so that the employer may pay the relevant remuneration without deducting tax.

Generally, where these deductions are claimed, the Inland Revenue are likely to scrutinise the arrangements to ensure that the remuneration paid is reasonable in relation to the duties performed and, in particular, that there is no 'loading' of remuneration against which a deduction is claimed as compared with that against which no deduction applies.

Now turning to the taxation of a *non-resident,* the basic rule is that a non-resident's employment earnings are taxed in the UK only insofar as they are attributable to any duties of that employment which are performed in this country. In instances where duties are carried out partly in this country and partly overseas, separate contracts of employment are strongly recommended. If duties are normally performed overseas, any duties performed in this country will still be treated as if they were performed overseas provided they are merely *incidental* to the overseas duties. A decision obviously has to be made as to what is classified as 'incidental': in general, it is not the time spent in this country which is the deciding factor, but if duties in this country occupy more than three months in a tax year, they cannot normally be said to be incidental. The Revenue will take into account the nature of the duties and their relationship to the overseas duties. (Again, remember that if any of the income is taxed in both countries it may be possible to claim double taxation relief–see question 25.) Personal reliefs for UK income tax are basically only available to a UK resident, but certain categories of non-residents can claim a proportion of them.

34 I have always lived abroad but now I have come to work in the UK: what is my tax position?

If you were born abroad and have always lived in that country your 'domicile' will generally be your country of origin as explained in the previous question. If you are *not domiciled in the UK but are resident and ordinarily resident* in this country (i.e. you are living here for six months or more in a tax year and you habitually live in this country), the general rules as to paying income tax are as follows: any income arising within the UK is chargeable to tax in full, and income arising outside the UK is chargeable to tax only by reference to the amounts which are remitted to the UK.

If the *employer is resident abroad* and *you, the employee, are domiciled abroad* your residence status may affect the way your earnings from that employer are taxed. If you are *resident and ordinarily resident* in the UK and have been since before 13th March 1984, *and* your job with the non-resident employer began before that date, income tax is only charged on 50% of those earnings; however, this deduction will *not* apply in 1984/85 or later years if you have been resident in the UK for at least nine out of the ten preceding years (previously in these circumstances, the relief was reduced to 25%). In any case, the 50% deduction will be reduced to 25% for the years 1987/88 and 1988/89 and thereafter withdrawn altogether.

The deduction will not be available at all if your job with the non-resident employer did not begin until after 13th March 1984, unless you took up duty in the UK before 1st August 1984 under a posting which had already been arranged on or before 13th March 1984.

It must be made clear that these rules do not apply to individuals who are employed by an employer resident in the Republic of Ireland; their earnings are specifically excluded from the relief.

A person who is resident in the UK may claim the personal allowances discussed in earlier questions.

35   Are there any other expenses I can claim?   ●

It cannot be emphasised too often that expenses are only allowable if they are incurred *wholly, exclusively and necessarily in the performance of the duties* of your employment. There must therefore be no question of the expenses being partly for your own benefit and they must be absolutely necessary for you to carry out your duties. Many of the claims made to the Revenue which fail, do so on the test of necessity.

You have already seen that the costs of travelling to work from home are generally not deductible because the costs are not incurred in the course of performing the duties, but in order to get to the place where the duties are to be performed. Travelling expenses *will* be allowed provided they are incurred wholly and exclusively in the performance of the duties of the office. It is generally accepted that travel expenses include the cost of accommodation while travelling.

You may wish to make a claim that part of your home is used as an office–this is covered in question 17. If, in addition to this, you purchase books, etc., you may find it difficult to prove that they are wholly, exclusively and necessarily for the performance of your duties. If you pay subscriptions to a *recognised* body, such as a professional institute, the amount you pay is an allowable expense.

Similarly, if you are a manual worker there are often fixed deductions agreed, depending on the actual nature of your employment and the industry in which you are employed.

3 NOW YOU ARE IN BUSINESS

TAXATION OF THE SELF-EMPLOYED

36 What happens when I start up in business?

Special rules apply for taxation purposes when a business first commences and when it ceases, otherwise tax would not be paid until a business was well under way, and would also be payable some time after it had ceased. Because of these rules tax savings are possible, if matters are timed correctly and the accounting date is chosen with care (see question 37).

It is important to determine the actual date on which a business commences as this also decides the first assessment for tax purposes. *The first assessment will tax the actual profits from the date the business started to the next 5th April* (i.e. end of the tax year). This will most probably mean the assessment is made on a proportion of the profits shown in the first accounts (computed on a time basis).

The second assessment will tax the profits of the first 12 months trading, from the date of commencement; however, if the first accounts are for a period of *less* than 12 months, the second and third years assessments will also be made on a time basis (which would most probably mean a proportion of the profit from the first two sets of accounts). If the *first accounts were prepared for a 12 month period* the third year's assessment will be based on the first accounts. This is called the *previous year basis of assessment* and will continue throughout the period of self-employment until the final year (i.e. the profits of your accounting period *ending* in the tax year 1986/87 will actually be *taxed* in 1987/88).

You do have an option that *all* the first three years of assessment be taxed on the actual profits for those years. This is only to be done if it is to your advantage (i.e. if the figures are smaller than those produced by the normal basis) and the election will normally only be made if the profits of the second and third accounting periods are lower than those earned in the first year of trading. Claims must be made within six years from the end of the third year of assessment.

If an election is not advantageous the first accounting period will be the basis for the first three years tax assessments, so it is important that the tax profits be kept as low as possible. If you consult your professional advisers they will suggest how this may be achieved.

In the following questions, general reference is made to 'trades' and 'trading', and exactly the same considerations are given to an individual carrying on a *profession* or *vocation*.

● **37 How do I choose my accounting date?**

Most people when left to their own devices will automatically prepare accounts for the first twelve months trading without seeking further advice: admittedly this has one advantage in enabling the first three years tax assessments to be settled earlier, but that is all. Other people prepare accounts for the calendar year or even the tax year. You should always consult a professional adviser before you choose your accounting date as there may be an advantage in your choosing a particular date depending on the line of business you are in. As a general guide, the date that has the most advantages is one early in the tax year (e.g. 30th April). You must remember that the choice of your accounting date is not so much a way of saving tax, but of deferring payment of that tax, and this is brought about due to the preceding year basis of assessment mentioned in the previous question.

As you have seen, the basis of assessment means that the profits you make during one year will not be taxed until the following year. To illustrate the point, the examples below use two different accounting dates–30th September and 30th April.

Examples

Ivor Crown, a dentist, makes up his accounts to 30th September.
Accounts to *30th September 1987:*
Profits taxable in *1988/89.*
Payment dates for tax in equal instalments:
1st January 1989,
1st July 1989.
The time lapse between the end of the accounting period and the due date of payment of the first instalment is *15 months.*

Orson Carte, the rag-and-bone man, makes up his accounts to 30th April.
Accounts to *30th April 1987:*
Profits taxable in *1988/89.*
Payment dates for tax in equal instalments:
1st January 1989,
1st July 1989.
The time lapse between the end of the accounting period and the due date for payment of the first instalment is *20 months.* Mr Carte therefore has 5 months extra time between the end of the accounting period and the due dates of payment. As pointed out previously, it will not save him tax but it may help his cash flow situation. (Refer to question 3 for details of when tax liabilities become due for payment.)

38 What happens if I change my accounting date? ●

If you are already in business and have a year end you think may not be giving you the best tax break, you may wish to consider changing your accounting date–no general advice can be given as each case *must* be examined separately. In many cases it may *not* be worthwhile because a change of accounting date means the basis of assessment of your· profits is affected and may result in increased tax liabilities; before any change is made it is essential to make detailed calculations for which you will require up-to-date accounts and accurate forecasts of trading, stock levels, etc.

If your profits have been reasonably static but an increase is likely in the future, it may be possible to obtain some saving of tax if you can move your accounting date from *late* in the tax year to *early* in the year. On the other hand, if profits have been high in the past and are now falling there may be scope for shortening the accounting period, especially if the original accounting date fell early in the tax year. The tax savings for this sort of venture may be large enough to make it a worthwhile exercise.

39 What happens when my business ceases? ●

The actual date of cessation is important (as for commencing in business) as this determines the final year of assessment. If you permanently discontinue your trade, the profits assessed in the final tax year are the *actual* profits earned from the start of that tax year (i.e.

6th April) to the date of cessation. You may remember that *you* have the option as to what is assessed in the second and third years of assessment–this time the *Revenue* have the option to revise the previous two years' assessments (i.e. the two years before the final year, which have both been assessed on a previous year basis) to assess the *profits actually earned* during the periods, calculated on a time basis. The Revenue will elect to do this if the total profits to be assessed on an 'actual' basis exceed the profits using the 'preceding year' basis.

Whichever basis is used, part of your profits will actually not be assessed at all but this is counteracted by the fact that your first trading profits will have been assessed more than once.

The timing of the cessation is important; each case requires careful consideration of its particular facts and an accurate estimate of profits to the date you propose to cease trading. A general rule is that where profits are falling the trade should cease prior to the start of the new tax year, but if profits are still rising it may be beneficial to cease early in the next tax year. In addition, there are special provisions relating to capital allowances (see question 43).

40   What can I do if I incur a loss in the first years of trading?

If you should be unfortunate enough to make a loss during any of the first four years of assessment from the date the trade commenced, you may make a claim that this loss be set off against your *other* income for the preceding three years, using the earlier years first. The Revenue will want you to show that the trade was carried on during the period the loss arose, on a *commercial basis,* with an expectation of profits in the near future, and you must make your claim within two years of the end of the year of assessment in which the loss occurred. The loss set off against your other income should give you a repayment of tax.

Alternatively, loss relief may be claimed under one of the ways described in question 41. Under certain circumstances it may be possible to use a combination of those reliefs.

41   What other ways are there of relieving losses?

If a loss has been sustained by you in the trade you are carrying on, this may be utilised in one of the following ways.

1 Set off losses against other income: A trading loss may be set off against your other income in the same year of assessment, or in the following year of assessment provided that the trade is still carried on in the later year.

A claim must be made within two years of the end of the year of assessment in question and the loss must be set off against your other earned income, followed by your unearned income, and then in turn against your spouse's earned and unearned income, unless you make a claim to exclude your spouse's income. Repayment of tax is then made accordingly.

There are further provisions if your loss is increased by claiming capital allowances, but no loss relief will be given unless the trade was carried on for the year in question on a commercial basis, with a view to realising a profit.

2 Carry-forward of losses against subsequent years' profits: If you claim relief under the above provisions you will receive the immediate benefit of a tax repayment, but you may decide it would be more beneficial to carry all your losses forward to a later year to be set against future profits from the *same trade*. You may claim your loss relief either by setting off the loss against your other income for the year, or carrying back the loss if it was incurred in the first years of trading, but you may still have a balance–this may be carried forward instead of the full amount. There is no time limit (except as regards unused stock relief) as to how many years the loss can be carried forward until it is completely used up, provided only that the same trade is still being carried on.

3 Carry-back of a terminal loss: A *terminal loss* is the amount of losses sustained in the *last 12 months of trading* when your business was permanently discontinued. These losses may be carried back and set off against the profits of your trade for the three years immediately prior to that in which the cessation occurred. Relief is given for the latest year first, then working backwards until the loss or the available profit is used up.

Beware of forfeiting your personal allowances. If your other income is low for the year in which you have a loss it may be covered by personal allowances. If this is the case do not claim for the loss to be used that year but carry it forward.

Remember, you can carry your losses forward but you *cannot* carry your personal allowances forward.

● 42 What can I claim as expenses?

Many people who are self-employed do not realise that the profit appearing in their accounts is not necessarily the same figure that will be assessed to tax. The accounts profit has to be adjusted for tax purposes as not all the expenses shown in the accounts are tax allowable. The basic rule is that *expenses are allowable if they are incurred wholly and exclusively for the purposes of the trade.* Thus it follows that if an expense was incurred partly for private purposes the whole of the expenditure will be disallowed as it does not fulfil the criterion of being wholly and exclusively for business purposes.

It would not be possible to set out all the allowable or disallowable expenses and your professional advisers will be able to tell you what you can or cannot claim. You must ensure that all the expenses you have incurred during a year are included in your accounts otherwise you may pay more tax than is necessary. Below is a list of some of the items most frequently seen in statements of expenses, with a note to say whether or not it is allowable expenditure for tax purposes.

Depreciation: Not allowable, but capital allowances may be claimed (see question 43).

Advertising: Generally allowable.

Remuneration: Allowable including bonuses, PAYE, cost of benefits provided, if relating to employees, not the proprietor.

Entertainment expenses: Not allowable, unless for staff or overseas customers. Disallowance similarly applies to business gifts.

Legal fees: Not allowable if incurred while acquiring a new asset as this is part of the capital cost. Generally allowable if it is the cost of maintaining existing trading assets and rights (e.g. debt collecting).

Personal expenses: Not allowable.

Rent, rates, etc., for business purposes: Allowable.

Income tax and NIC payable/paid: Not allowable (except on employees' pay).

Subscriptions: Allowable if to trade or professional association or for trade publications.

Donations: Donations to charities are allowable provided the 'wholly and exclusively' rule is satisfied (i.e. there is a business or trade connection).

Travelling and subsistence: Allowable if in the course of the business activities. Not allowable are travelling expenses between home and the business address.

Repairs and renewals: Expenditure on additions, alterations or improvements is capital and not allowable. Repairs (i.e. restoring something to its original condition, etc.) are allowable.

Leasing: Generally allowable in full where assets used wholly and exclusively for business purposes. Exceptionally a restriction is applied for motor cars costing more than £8,000 when new.

Telephone: Business use only allowable.

Where any such expenditure is incurred in connection with a new business in the three years prior to the commencement of trading, it may also be claimed as a deduction in the first year's tax assessment.

You will appreciate it is easier for a self-employed person to claim expenses in respect of his work than for an employee, whose claim may fail on the grounds it is not a 'necessary' expense–as you have seen earlier (question 35).

Recently, considerable interest was aroused in a case where a lady barrister tried to claim a deduction for tax purposes for the special dark clothes that she was required to wear in court. Eventually the House of Lords ruled against her on the grounds that she was not able to establish that she had bought the clothes concerned *exclusively* for the purposes of her profession: she also had to meet the personal requirements of decency and warmth!

43 What is the effect for tax purposes of capital expenditure?

If you incur expenses by acquiring a capital asset you may not deduct this from your trading profit. Assuming that the asset has a limited life span, its value to your business will gradually decline and this is anticipated by including in the accounts an amount for depreciation, but this in itself is not allowable for tax purposes. Instead there are specific allowances available against certain types of capital expenditure, as noted below.

Machinery and plant
Industrial buildings
Agricultural land and buildings
Mines, oil wells and mineral deposits
Dredging
Scientific research
Patents
Know-how
Cemeteries

The first three of these categories (being the most common) are dealt with in more detail below.

It may be that a particular item of capital expenditure falls into more than one category and you would normally be able to state your preference which will obviously be to your advantage, but there are special provisions which restrict this choice in certain contexts. You must make a claim to the Revenue for the allowances but you will see it is not always advantageous to claim them. In general, the granting of the allowances falls into three stages:

1 An *initial or first year allowance* of a substantial percentage of the capital expenditure: it is possible for you to claim only part of this but it would depend on the particular circumstances as to whether or not you did so. As will be seen below, these allowances have been largely phased out so as no longer to apply for expenditure incurred after 31st March 1986.

2 A *writing down allowance* each year during the life of the asset (see later notes).

3 A *balancing charge or allowance* at the end of the trade or on the disposal of the asset. This is to bring the allowances into line with the actual amount spent, i.e. the difference between original cost and the proceeds of disposal: if the amount given as an allowance is less than the amount spent the difference is a *balancing allowance;* if the allowance exceeds the amount spent, the difference is brought into the income tax assessment by way of a *balancing charge.* (If the asset is sold at a profit the amount brought back into charge will not exceed the original allowances given: the excess may be charged to CGT–see Chapter 5.)

The allowance is normally set against your taxable profits but if you have a loss the capital allowances can be used to increase the loss or turn a small profit into a loss. A word of advice–remember you cannot carry forward your personal allowances and you must consider whether or not you wish to claim the full first year allowance (for treatment of losses see questions 40 and 41).

Machinery and plant: This is certainly the most common of the capital allowances claims but as there is no definition of machinery or plant in the legislation it has provoked much discussion through the years. It includes *fixtures and fittings* but recently the Revenue has been taking a much stricter view as to what qualifies; it depends on the relation of the fixture in the building and whether or not it is used for the trade. One example, taken from a recent tax case, is where special lighting and wall decorations were installed in a number of pubs to improve the atmosphere. It was held that because of the contribution that these fittings made to the development of business, they could be treated as fixtures and fittings, and so qualify for capital allowances, rather than as part of the 'setting' in which the trade was carried out.

The terms 'machinery' and 'plant' also include *motor vehicles* and these are dealt with in question 44. A few of the other rules concerning plant and machinery are as follows.

First year allowances: For expenditure incurred on or before 13th March 1984 it was possible to claim an allowance equal to 100% of the expenditure. This also applies to expenditure incurred up to 31st March 1987 where there was a binding contract already entered into on or before 13th March 1984. Otherwise for expenditure incurred after the latter date, the amount of the possible first year allowance was reduced to the following.

Between 14th March 1984 and	
31st March 1985 inclusive	75%
Between 1st April 1985 and	
31st March 1986 inclusive	50%
After 31st March 1986	Nil

As indicated above you do not have to claim the full amount of this allowance if you do not wish to do so.

Writing down allowances: If 100% first year allowance is claimed then this is not applicable. All plant and machinery used in the trade is grouped together into a 'pool' (but see question 44 regarding motor vehicles). For the first year it is claimed, the allowance will be

25% of cost or the amount remaining following first year allowance. The net figure of the cost less the allowance is called the *written down value*–in the following year an allowance is given of 25% of this figure and the same procedure is repeated in subsequent years.

Leasing: No first year allowance, if purchased after 1st June 1980, except in certain circumstances.

Hire purchase: First year allowance on capital element at the beginning of contract–no need to wait for instalments to be paid.

Industrial buildings

General rules are as follows:
1 Building must be an industrial building or structure–defined in great detail in the legislation.
2 Claimant may be a trader or a landlord, but the expenditure *must* be incurred on the construction of 'an industrial building or structure which is to be occupied *for the purposes of a trade'*.
3 Cost of land is excluded; private roads are included as a concession.
4 Special rules where only part of the building qualifies, where expenditure was incurred before 1962 and when the building is sold.
5 Special rules and allowances for hotels, for commercial buildings in 'enterprise zones' and (until 26th March 1985) for 'small workshops'.
6 Initial allowance depending on when expenditure was incurred, are as follows.

On or before 13th March 1984	75%
Between 14th March 1984 and 31st March 1985 inclusive	50%
Between 1st April 1985 and 31st March 1986 inclusive	25%
After 31st March 1986	Nil

Writing down allowance of 4% of cost until fully written off.

Agricultural land and buildings

General rules are as follows:
1 Expenditure must be incurred for husbandry or forestry–proportion of the allowance can be given where appropriate.
2 Claimant may be the landlord or tenant of any agricultural or forestry land who incurs expenditure on construction of

farmhouses, farm or forestry buildings, cottages, fences or other works (e.g. water supplies, drainage).

3 Apportionment of allowance applies when expenditure is on a farmhouse–one-third is allowable.

4 Expenditure incurred on or before 31st March 1986: initial allowance 20% ; writing down allowance 10% of cost for eight years. Expenditure incurred after 31st March 1986: initial allowance Nil; writing down allowance 4% of cost for 25 years.

5 Special rules apply when the building is sold.

44 What is the tax position on buying motor cars? If I use my own car can I claim tax allowances?

As you have already seen, motor vehicles are classed as plant and machinery but only certain types qualify for the 100% first year allowance. These are goods vehicles (e.g. lorries), vehicles unsuitable to be used as private vehicles (or not commonly used as such) and vehicles which are provided wholly or mainly for hire to the general public. If it is decided not to claim the whole of the first year allowance, the vehicles will be included in the 'pool' and the 25% writing down allowance will be granted (both these terms are explained in the 'Machinery and plant' section of the previous question).

There is no first year allowance on other motor cars but if the car is bought by the business and you use it during the course of your business, the 25% writing down allowance will be granted with the car put into a separate 'pool', unless it cost more than £8,000. If this is the case the writing down allowance is restricted to £2,000 each year, until the amount brought forward falls below £8,000 when the 25% rate of allowance becomes applicable.

If all the car expenses have been claimed in the accounts and these include private motoring expenses, an adjustment will be made to the taxable profit as you are not entitled to tax allowances for the private use of your car. If you use your own car for business purposes, again you may claim the writing down allowance and running expenses but they will be restricted to the business proportion only. Finally, remember that when the car is sold (whether it is owned by the business or yourself), if you have been claiming writing down allowances, an adjustment will be made in the form of a balancing allowance or charge as explained in the previous question.

45   As a self-employed person, what provision can I make towards my retirement?

You are entitled to claim all the same personal allowances whether you are self-employed or an employee. There is one relief, however, which cannot be claimed by any person who holds a pensionable office or employment (i.e. he is an employee in an approved superannuation scheme which provides for his retirement).

The allowance referred to is *Retirement Annuity Relief* which not only saves you tax but also provides you with a pension when you retire, normally between the ages of 60 and 75.

You are entitled to deduct from your 'net relevant earnings' as assessed for a tax year, any premium paid under a Revenue approved annuity contract. The term *net relevant earnings* means your earnings from your self-employment (or non-pensionable employment) having taken into account losses, stock relief and capital allowances.

You are allowed to claim a certain percentage of your net relevant earnings as a qualifying premium, depending on when you were born. Currently the rates are as follows.

Year of Birth	Percentage
1934 or later	17.5%
1916–1933	20%
1914–1915	21%
1912–1913	24%

This relief will normally be given against income in the tax year in which the premium is paid, but it is possible to elect for a premium to be treated as paid in the previous year, or if there were no relevant earnings in that year, in the next preceding year of assessment.

It may also be possible to make use of 'unused relief' from earlier years. Where the maximum amount of relief which would be available exceeds the premium paid in a year, the excess is to be treated as unused relief: this may be carried forward for up to six years and used when the reverse situation arises and the premiums paid exceed the amount allowable. Relief given in this way must be taken in the earliest possible year. *In general,* the rule to remember is that it is possible to take up unused relief before the end of six years, but that it is lost when the six year period comes to an end. However, it is possible by using the 'relating back' rules mentioned above to obtain an extension. For instance, unused relief for 1980/81 should strictly be forfeited by 5th April 1987 but if a payment were to be made in the following year 1987/88, it could be related back to 1986/87 and then unused relief for 1980/81 could be set against any excess premiums in that year. (Taking the example a step further, if there were no relevant earnings in 1986/87 the payment could be related back to 1985/86 and thus take advantage of unused relief from 1979/80, which would normally have been forfeited at 5th April 1986!)

One other point concerning retirement annuity relief is the 'loan-back' facility. In the past, one of the disadvantages of paying into a pension scheme was the fact that money was paid in and was not seen again until the date of retirement. Facilities are now offered by a number of life assurance companies which allow you to borrow back an amount up to the level of the premiums paid, which means that the only cost need be the interest on the loan, which is charged at a commercial rate. The loan will be repaid when the policy matures, either out of the funds of the pension itself or your own personal funds.

46 Are there any businesses which have special rules?

No matter what trade, profession or vocation you are engaged in, you will find differences, particularly in relation to the expenses which are allowable, but there are certain categories which are set apart in the legislation for special treatment. Three of these categories are discussed very briefly below.

1 Subcontractors in the construction industry: The main thing to remember in this instance is that unless you hold a subcontractor's exemption certificate you will have basic rate tax deducted from all the payments you receive for your work. This tax is then available as a credit when an agreement concerning your tax is eventually reached, so the main disadvantage is with regard to your cash flow situation, which could be of major importance. In order to obtain a certificate, you must keep all your income tax returns, accounts and payments of tax up to date as all these things are examined closely before the issue of a certificate is authorised; some of these requirements may be relaxed in the case of school or college leavers who are newly starting in the industry.

2 Farmers: Basically the rules of assessment are the same as for any other self-employed person but there are a few notable differences:
Losses–unlike other trades, all farming (but not market gardening)

is treated as *one* trade so that a loss on one farm may be set off against the profit on another. However, it is not possible to set farming losses against other income for the same year or a succeeding year of assessment (see question 41) if losses were also incurred in farming in each of the five years preceding the year of assessment concerned, except in certain circumstances.

Capital allowances–special reliefs for agricultural land and buildings (see question 43).

Treatment of livestock–generally animals kept by a farmer are to be treated as trading stock. Where animals such as these form part of a production herd the farmer may elect for them to be treated as a capital asset–*herd basis*. (If you think this applies to your livestock–seek further advice.)

Fluctuating profits–complicated rules apply, but a good way of saving tax if the tests are met. Relief is by way of averaging two years' profits where there is a difference between the two years of more than 25% of the higher figure.

3 Landowners: Landowners who are not carrying on a trade are taxed on rent less expenses and this net figure is treated as unearned income, unless they meet the special tests relating to *furnished holiday accommodation* (see question 24). There are also what are called 'one estate' provisions in that expenses incurred on one property may be set against the rents arising on another within the same 'estate' provided that certain conditions are satisfied.

● **47   What is the position if I am in partnership?**

First of all it must be shown that there is actually a partnership: *an agreement to trade together and share the profits or losses* is presumed to be a partnership. The agreement does not have to be a formal legal document (in fact it can be made orally), but it is preferable to have the terms written down in some form.

Where there is a partnership, income tax is assessed on the profits of the trade or profession in the name of the partnership, although in England and Wales a partnership is not a legal entity. *Each partner is jointly liable for income tax on the whole of the profits*. Where a partnership includes a company, special rules are needed because a company, unlike an individual, is always taxed on the current year's profits, i.e. no preceding year basis of assessment.

The rules concerning the allocation of profits from a partnership are rather involved. The partners agree for each accounting year how the accounts profit is to be divided between them–this is called the *profit sharing ratio*. However, the same profit is not necessarily divided up in the same way for tax purposes. This is because the profit sharing ratio for the income tax assessment is the ratio actually in use for that tax year and due to the preceding years basis of assessment the accounts profits for one year are not assessed until the following year, by which time the partners may have agreed to allocate their current profits differently, as shown in the following example.

Example

John, Paul and Peter are in partnership. They make up their accounts to 31st March each year. The accounts to 31st March 1987 show a taxable profit of £36,000 which is divided *equally* between them. This profit will be taxed in 1987/88 (the tax year ended 5th April 1988).

Shortly after the start of their new accounting period it is decided that because John works so hard he is to have one-half of the current year's profit (to 31st March 1988) while Paul and Peter will now take only one-quarter each.

The income tax assessment for 1987/88 is based on the profits to 31st March 1987 (£36,000) but it is divided using the profit sharing ratio for the current year, to 31st March 1988. The assessment is therefore divided up as follows.

Total profit £36,000		
	John –	£18,000
	Paul –	£9,000
	Peter –	£9,000

However, each partner is actually entitled to £12,000 for the year concerned. It may be possible to turn this sort of situation to your advantage with careful planning and professional advice.

Partners' salaries and interest on capital are not an allowable expense for income tax purposes, being regarded as an element of the partnership profits.

48   What happens if there is a change in the partnership?

In the event of any change in the partners, for tax purposes the business is automatically assumed to have ceased and a new business started at the date of the change: this brings into operation special provisions relating to commencement and cessation. So far as the 'old partnership' is concerned, the rules described in question 39 apply. As regards the 'new partnership', up to 19th March 1985 the provisions set out in question 36 applied; for partnership changes taking place after that date, the partnership is assessed to tax on its actual profits for the first *four* years with the normal previous year basis only applying in the fifth and subsequent years. There is still an option to have the fifth and sixth years assessed on an actual basis if this is to the partners' advantage.

But if there is one partner (at least) who is a partner both before and after the change it is possible to elect for the *continuing basis of assessment* to apply. The election must be signed by all the partners both before and after the change (or, in the case of a deceased partner, by an executor) and the claim must be made within two years of the date of the change–it can also be revoked during this time. It must be emphasised that the Revenue are very strict in the application of this particular time limit.

The effect of the election will be for the profits to be assessed on the normal preceding year basis, the year of change being apportioned between the 'old' and 'new' partnerships on a time basis.

It is often beneficial to make the election and the necessary calculations should always be made to ensure that as little tax as possible is payable. It is essential to seek professional advice on this matter.

● **49   Part of my business is carried on abroad: can I claim any tax deduction for this?**

Generally, profits arising from self-employed trades or professional earnings are charged to UK tax in full, irrespective of where they arise.

Up to 5th April 1985, a limited form of relief was available where some part of the business activities were carried on abroad. This was similar to the relief for short absences abroad for employees described in question 33 and like that relief has been withdrawn altogether after 5th April 1985.

If you are *not domiciled,* though *resident,* you will be liable to tax only on *remittances* of income to the UK from the overseas business. If you are *not resident and not ordinarily resident* then you are not liable to UK tax on such earnings.

50   Should I consider turning my business into a company?

There are several advantages to be obtained from incorporating a business but there are also many problems to be overcome. You may have derived substantial income tax benefits from the opening years of assessment rules and the special relief for losses in the early years of trading. If the profits of your business increase rapidly, making the idea of incorporating your business a good one, the additional income tax payable when adjustments are made to the closing years of assessment, together with professional fees and capital costs of starting the company, may well exceed the initial tax savings. There may be other non-tax reasons why incorporation is attractive (e.g. product liability claims). On the other hand, incorporation does not always give effective protection of limited liability (e.g. a personal guarantee to a bank), and matters such as these must be taken into consideration.

You should first of all consult with your professional adviser to discuss what would be the most suitable form of trading vehicle for your particular business. The reduction in income tax rates, and the higher level of NICs payable by employer and employee, compared with the contributions paid by the self-employed, have made the decision to incorporate more difficult as the tax aspect is less obviously attractive.

Let us look at the main advantages and disadvantages in more detail.

Advantages

1 You would be able to establish a company pension scheme (subject to approval by the Inland Revenue). The contributions paid by the company and the employee are tax deductible and are usually greater than the amounts allowable for retirement annuity premiums (see questions 13 and 46). The benefits are also generally more attractive.

2 You may be able to make gifts of shares to utilise the annual IHT exemptions (see question 88). The CGT position should not be overlooked but it may be possible to keep the chargeable gain below the taxable limit or take advantage of the holdover relief available for gifts (see question 72).

3 It may be easier for you to raise additional finance from banks and other third parties.

4 The benefit of limited liability can be obtained which can give valuable protection against financial risks, product liability claims and so on.

Disadvantages

1 Additional accounting and audit requirements are imposed on companies.

2 You may lose some of the flexibility of your previous business arrangements. You will be required to maintain minutes of directors meetings and other general meetings and to comply with the statutory filing requirements, the most important one being to file a copy of the accounts with the Companies Registration Office each year. Such filed accounts are available for inspection by any member of the public.

3 Once you become a director of a company rather than a participant in an unincorporated business (whether by yourself or in partnership) you are then subject to the stricter rules concerning benefits and expenses, and your drawings from the company are subject to PAYE–which can cause cash flow problems.

4 If you have a husband and wife partnership with a flexible profit sharing agreement this will have to cease if the business is incorporated. The agreement may have meant your spouse was given a material slice of the profits, to utilise personal allowances and the lower rates of tax, although he or she perhaps did not take a very active part in the business. Once the business becomes a company any remuneration paid instead will be reviewed by the Inland Revenue more critically and if it is considered to be excessive for the duties actually undertaken, the Inspector may not allow a part of the salary paid to be deducted for corporation tax purposes.

● **51   How does incorporation actually affect my income tax position?**

The transfer of your business to a company is treated as a cessation of the unincorporated business and the special rules for the final years of trading will apply (see question 39). The timing of the incorporation therefore requires careful planning if increased income tax assessments are to be avoided.

There are special rules concerning capital allowances and losses. These are complicated but can be used to produce some saving in tax. The incorporation of a business is something you should *not* consider without professional advice.

4 KEEPING GOOD COMPANY

TAXATION OF THE COMPANY–CORPORATION TAX

52 What are the basic rules of corporation tax (including rates of tax, reliefs, dates for payments, etc.)?

The first and perhaps the most obvious rule, is that corporation tax is only paid by companies. A company means any *body corporate or unincorporated association* but does not include a partnership, a local authority or a local authority association. There are special rules and exemptions for certain types of companies, including charitable companies, unregistered friendly societies, trade unions, scientific research associations, and for certain nationalised industries.

To be liable to pay corporation tax a company must be *resident* in the UK and it will then pay tax on all its profits, wherever they arise. The residence of a company does not necessarily depend on where the trade is carried on: it is resident where it is controlled and managed on a day-to-day basis. This may be determined by the place where the main board of directors makes executive decisions in the running of the company; however, this test is not conclusive. The country of residence of the directors or the shareholders is not relevant. *Non-resident* companies are only subject to corporation tax if they are carrying on a trade through a branch or agency in the UK; but if this is the case, they are then taxable on the profits arising from that branch or agency.

Unlike income tax assessments on individuals and sole traders, corporation tax is not complicated by the preceding year basis of assessment. Corporation tax is assessed on a company for its *accounting period*. The accounting period for tax purposes is normally the same as the company's period of account: it is sometimes necessary to determine an accounting period in instances where the company commences or ceases to trade in a period of account, or the period of account is longer than a year. An accounting period for tax purposes *cannot* exceed 12 months, so where the company prepares its accounts for a period of more than 12 months there will be two accounting periods, one for 12 months and the other for the balance, the profits being allocated on a time basis. If, therefore, the company has an 18 month period of account, there will be an assessment raised on the first 12 months on two-thirds of the profit, and a further assessment for the other six months on one-third of the profit.

Corporation tax is assessed, not for the income tax year ended 5th April, but for the *financial year to 31st March*. If an accounting period straddles that date, the profits have to be apportioned between two financial years and taxed accordingly.

The rates of corporation tax currently fixed are 35% for the years ended 31st March 1987 and 1988. These rates apply where the annual profits exceed £500,000.

A *small companies rate* applies where the annual profits do not exceed £100,000; this has been set at 29% for the year ended 31st March 1987 and at 27% for the year ending 31st March 1988. There is a marginal relief available where the profits fall between £100,000 and £500,000.

The tax is normally due nine months after the end of the accounting period, or if the assessment is made late within 30 days of the date the assessment is issued. There is an exception to this rule for companies which were trading on 1st April 1964, when they were still paying income tax. They will continue to have the same interval from their accounting date to the due date for payment, as they did under the old income tax rules. This concession is being phased out over the next three years so that *all* companies will be on a nine month payment date.

If the tax is paid late the risk is run of incurring an *interest charge* as for income tax (see question 3), but on the other hand if there is a corporation tax refund due from the Inland Revenue, if certain tests are satisfied there may be a *repayment supplement* due, again with similar rules to income tax.

You may have heard the term *close company* which is applied to a company that is controlled by five (or fewer) of the main shareholders, or by its directors. (This is over-simplifying the position–the rules to decide whether a company is close or not are very complicated.) Formerly, the legislation was such that if a company was close it could lead to problems as the law required a certain amount of the income of these companies to be distributed each year, and there was also a much wider view of what constituted a distribution made by the company. However, recent legislation has greatly relaxed the rules relating to *close trading companies,* so that these companies should not normally have any problem in the future.

53 What are the profits of a company? Are they computed in the same way as for income tax? ●

The *profits* of a company include both *income* and *chargeable gains.* The amount of income is, in general, computed in accordance with income tax principles as described in questions 42 to 44. The taxation of chargeable gains is dealt with separately (see question 57).

A company is not entitled to personal reliefs and allowances as these are only available to individuals.

Special rules apply to what are called *charges on income* which comprise chiefly of annual interest (but not bank interest), royalties and payments under charitable deeds of covenant (see question 54). They are allowed as deductions against the *total profits* of the accounting period in which they are *actually paid.* Interest payable to a bank is generally treated as a trading expense and not as a charge on income.

Charges on income must be paid under deduction of income tax at the basic rate and the company must pay this tax over to the Collector of Taxes (unless a group situation applies–see question 63).

Where there are charges on income consisting of payments made wholly and exclusively for the purposes of a trade carried on by the company, and these plus other charges on income exceed the total profits of the company, then whichever is the *smaller* of the charges incurred exclusively for the trade or the excess of charges over profit is treated as a trading expense and so entitled to *loss relief.* Losses incurred in this way can only be carried forward, they cannot be carried back to a previous accounting period.

54 Can a company obtain relief for donations to charity? ●

Although not generally qualifying as a business expense, by specific provision in the legislation, a company may obtain relief for corporation tax purposes for payments made under a deed of covenant to a charity, similar to the relief described in question 22.

As for an individual, the term of the deed must be capable of exceeding three years. As mentioned in the previous question, the payments must be made under deduction of income tax at the basic rate which must be paid over to the Collector of Taxes. However, the charity can then reclaim this tax, so effectively receiving the covenanted payment gross; the company will in the meantime be able to claim the *gross* amount of the payments as a deduction in arriving at its corporation tax liability. The working of this is illustrated in the following example.

Example

Scrooge Ltd covenants by deed to pay the Tiny Tim Charity an annual amount of £100 for four years.

Scrooge Ltd makes the following payments each year.

	£
To the Charity £100 less tax at 27%	73
Income tax withheld, paid over to Collector of Taxes	27
	100
Corporation tax relief at 35% (say)	35
Net cost to Scrooge Ltd	£ 65

The charity receives the following amounts:

From Scrooge Ltd	73
By repayment from the Inland Revenue	27
Total income under deed	£100

As part of the present Government's policy to provide further support and encouragement for charitable giving, a new relief for companies (other than close companies, see question 52) has been brought in with effect from 1st April 1986. This allows companies to obtain tax relief for one-off gifts to charity, up to a maximum equal to 3% of the ordinary dividends paid by the company. This relief operates in the same way as that described for charitable covenants, with the paying company deducting basic rate income tax from the payments made and accounting for that tax to the Revenue; the charity recovers the tax as before.

55 Can my company claim allowances for capital expenditure in the same way as an individual or partnership?

Again, the rules for claiming capital allowances are much the same as for individuals and partnerships (see question 43). There is *one important difference,* in that if losses are increased or actually arise from claiming a *first year allowance* in respect of plant or machinery, the trading loss arising from such a claim can be carried back up to *three years* (which generally would lead to the re-opening of an earlier year and a repayment of corporation tax). With the phasing out of first year allowances mentioned in question 43, this relief is now becoming obsolete.

56 If my company incurs losses, how can they be utilised?

Where a trading loss arises in a company there are a number of ways in which relief for it may be obtained:

1 The trading loss may be carried forward to be set against future profits from the *same trade.*

2 Alternatively, the trading loss may be set against other profits of the same period, including chargeable gains.

3 The loss may be carried back for one year and set against profits from all sources provided the company was trading during that period.

4 Losses may be carried back for up to three years if created by a claim for first year allowances (see question 55).

5 Trading losses incurred by a company which is a member of a group can be passed to another member of the group (see question 63).

6 Trading losses incurred in the last 12 months of trading (i.e. a terminal loss) can be carried back for up to three years.

7 Allowable expenditure incurred in the three years before trading commenced may be claimed as an expense in the first accounting period.

57 What is the CGT position of a company?

The profits of a company which are chargeable to corporation tax include its chargeable gains after setting off its losses. For disposals of assets made on or after 17th March 1987 the gains are to be charged at the appropriate rate, i.e. the normal rate of 35% or the small companies rate of 29% or 27%, as applicable.

For disposals made before 17th March 1987 a different arrangement applied; effectively, a company paid tax on its chargeable gains at the same rate as an individual, i.e. 30%. To achieve this only a proportion of the gains was charged to tax but always at the normal rate; thus for a corporation tax rate of 35%, six-sevenths of the gains were chargeable to tax (see question 52).

If a company incurs a trading loss it may carry the losses forward against future trading profits, or the loss can be set against profits of the same accounting period, no matter what the description; a *trading loss may therefore be set off against chargeable gains of the same accounting period.* However, the reverse cannot happen–a capital loss cannot be set against trading profits but can only be set against current or future capital gains. In addition, chargeable gains cannot be used to relieve trading losses brought forward nor a terminal loss carried back (see question 56).

Remember, the company may also claim rollover relief (see question 79).

58   What are the tax consequences if my company pays a dividend?

Persons owning shares in a profitable company may look for some return on their investment in the form of a periodic dividend on their shares. This is usually paid yearly or half-yearly and the amount will depend on what the directors consider is available out of the profits of the company for distribution in this way. This can apply particularly where some of the shareholders are not directors and therefore draw no remuneration from the company; otherwise it is not uncommon for family private companies not to pay any dividends at all (though this can sometimes lead to problems with non-trading companies or companies with substantial investment, as distinct from trading, income).

If your company pays a dividend it is also required to make a payment of *advance corporation tax* (ACT) to the Revenue within certain time limits. The name derives from the fact that the company is entitled to offset payments of ACT against its liability to corporation tax on its profits, primarily those of the accounting period in which the dividend is paid. This set off may be subject to certain restrictions and to the extent that it cannot be fully used then, the surplus may be carried back for relief for a period of up to six years or carried forward indefinitely.

The purpose of the tax is to ensure that the dividend can be treated as income in the hands of the recipient which has already suffered tax. Thus when the shareholder receives his net dividend he is also regarded as being entitled to a 'tax credit' (equivalent to the corresponding ACT) which is taken into account in his own tax settlement. Up to 5th April 1987, the rate of ACT was 29/71sts of the amount of the dividend paid, corresponding to the basic rate of income tax of 29% on the 'gross equivalent', i.e. the dividend plus tax credit. From 6th April 1987, the rate of ACT is 27/73rds, corresponding to the basic rate fixed for 1987/88 of 27%. The operation of this may be illustrated as follows.

Example

Norah Bone Ltd is a company specialising in the sale of canned dog food. In the year ended 31st March 1987 the company made taxable profits of £600,000; on 31st July 1986 it paid a dividend of £71,000 to its shareholders.

Its corporation tax position for the year would be:

	£
Profits chargeable to corporation tax	600,000
Corporation tax at 35%	210,000
Dividend paid	71,000
ACT thereon at 29/71sts	29,000
(= 29% of £71,000 + £29,000)	

The company would actually account for its corporation tax liability in two parts.

	£
ACT due 14.10.86	29,000
Balance ('mainstream liability') due 1.1.88	181,000
	£210,000

If a shareholder received out of this dividend £7,100 he would be entitled to a tax credit of 29/71sts of £7,100, i.e. £2,900. If, because of other income, he is effectively liable to income tax at a rate of

60% on this income, he would have additional tax (known as 'excess liability') of £3,100 to pay for the tax year 1986/87, calculated as follows.

	£
'Gross equivalent', i.e. £7,100 + £2,900	10,000
Income tax thereon, at 60%	6,000
Less tax credit	2,900
	£3,100

This further tax would be due on 1st December 1987 or 30 days after the issue of the notice of assessment if this is later (see question 2).

On the other hand, if the shareholder was not liable to tax at all on this income, for example because it was a charity, then it could reclaim the whole of the tax credit of £2,900 from the Inland Revenue.

The question has referred only to *dividends*. However, there are other categories of payments in money or money's worth called *distributions* which are liable to ACT in the same way. In particular where shareholders take assets, e.g. stock in trade, out of the company at less than market value, the undervalue is taxed as if it were a dividend. A similar result follows where shareholders put assets into a company at an overvalue. Transfers between a company and its shareholders do therefore need to be looked at carefully with this aspect in mind.

Where a company receives a dividend (or distribution) from another UK company, it is *not* liable to any corporation tax on that dividend. However, it cannot use the tax credit that goes with that dividend, except against any liability to ACT on dividends that it in turn pays. A set off in this way does reduce the eventual amount available for credit against the company's corporation tax liability.

● **59 As a director and shareholder of a company, should I draw remuneration or dividends from the company?**

When investment income was generally subject to higher rates of tax than earned income, the best practice was for an individual to draw remuneration from his company rather than dividends. However, the abolition of the investment income surcharge (see question 2) has removed that bias against investment income and there are now a variety of factors which need to be taken into account. The most appropriate answer depends very much on the particular circumstances of the company and of the individuals concerned and no decision in this area should be taken without the benefit of proper professional advice.

However, here are some of the considerations that need to be borne in mind.

1 An individual may claim his personal allowances etc. against dividend income as well as against earned income (e.g. remuneration).

2 Pension scheme contributions can only be paid where there is a source of earned income, whether through an occupational scheme or a personal pension scheme (see question 13).

3 No national insurance contributions are payable on dividends; this could represent a real saving as compared with the Class 1 contributions due by both the individual and the company in respect of remuneration (see question 14). On the other hand, there could be some loss of benefit if the full contributions are not kept up.

4 Remuneration is normally paid under PAYE, with the appropriate relief for allowances and deductions being given (see question 27) but with any liability to higher rate tax being collected at the same time.

Dividends are effectively paid out under deduction of basic rate tax only, leaving any higher rate tax to be collected from the recipient later, as described in question 58.

5 It is possible to pay remuneration in arrears, for example by way of a bonus, some time after the year end when the company's results for the year are known, and relate this back so as to rank as a further deduction against that year's profits. Care needs to be taken in dealing with amounts that may have already been drawn by way of 'advances' in this situation, as under certain circumstances these can lead to further tax liabilities arising on the company or on the individual.

It is not possible to relate back a dividend payment in this way and the corresponding ACT has to be relieved primarily against corporation tax on the profits of the accounting period in which the dividend is paid.

6 Income tax withheld under PAYE and national insurance contributions have to be accounted for to the Revenue on a *monthly* basis. ACT only has to be accounted for every quarter.

7 Where a company has established a pattern of paying dividends, this could affect adversely any valuation that has to be agreed with the Inland Revenue on a transfer of its shares in connection with a tax planning scheme for its shareholders, so possibly leading to an increased charge to inheritance tax (see question 91).

8 To avoid any challenge by the Revenue as to its deductibility in the company's accounts, it is advisable to maintain remuneration at a reasonable level commensurate with the duties performed by the directors concerned.

In any event, whether money is drawn as remuneration or dividend, it will be sensible to try to bring the company's rate of tax and your own together as near as possible. As explained in question 52, after 31st March 1987 a company pays tax at present at a rate of between 27% and 35% depending on its level of profits. You start paying tax (after allowances and deductions) in 1987/88 at 27%; as shown in question 1, this rises to 40% for taxable income over £17,900 and to a maximum of 60% above £41,200.

If the company is incurring trading losses, there may be little point in paying out any remuneration, except to the extent necessary to enable the directors to use all their personal allowances; once these have been lost, they cannot be picked up in a later year.

Remember that where a company is making losses there may be restrictions under company law as to how much, if anything, may be paid out as dividends.

● **60   How can I provide my employees with a stake in the company in a tax efficient way?**

An individual who works for a company which is successful or which he believes is going to be successful is often interested in acquiring an interest in that company and so participating in its success in the longer term. By the same token, the directors of the company may see this as a way of providing their employees with an added incentive to stay with the company and make their own contribution to its success. This may be difficult, particularly if the company is an unquoted one with no market for its shares.

Basically, it must be recognised that where an employee acquires shares in his employer company other than for their full price, this is in effect an addition to his remuneration and the 'benefit' that he acquires is to be taxed accordingly. Indeed, the legislation goes further and aims to tax, under certain circumstances, as earned income the subsequent appreciation in value of those shares; the results can be quite penal.

However, there are certain arrangements sanctioned by the legislation which allow these provisions to be avoided and permit employees to acquire shares in their employer company on advantageous terms without being severely taxed. The provisions are very complex and expert professional advice is essential; what follows is only a brief summary of the current law and practice in this area. It should be emphasised that all those schemes require the approval of the Inland Revenue which must be obtained in advance.

Profit related pay (PRP)

A major initiative was announced by the Chancellor in his Budget speech on 17th March 1987 (although it had been foreshadowed in the 1986 Budget) to bring in a tax-based incentive whereby employees would be encouraged to take part of their remuneration by sharing in the company's profits. It is proposed that one-half of PRP will be free of income tax up to the point where PRP forms 20% of an employee's pay or £3,000 per annum, whichever is lower. It is anticipated that a married man on average earnings would receive relief amounting to approximately £6 per week. PRP will be subject to national insurance contributions in the usual way. All private sector employees will be eligible to receive relief except controlling directors. The employer must register with the Revenue the PRP scheme before it comes into operation. The PRP scheme must relate to an identifiable 'employment unit' which could be the whole business or a sub-unit of it.

Employers will generally be free to design their own schemes but certain basic qualifications will be required.

1 There will have to be a clear relationship between the PRP of the employment unit and its audited profits.

2 New recruits and part-timers may be excluded. Otherwise, at least 80% of the employees within the employment unit can be covered by the PRP scheme.

3 When the scheme commences, it must be seen to anticipate that where profits remain the same, the total PRP produced by the formula under point 1 will be at least 5% of the participating employees' total pay.

4 The scheme must run for at least one year.

Obviously, any decision to implement a PRP scheme has to be made by the employer, probably after consultation with his employees. It is suggested that a scheme could be introduced into pay bargains instead of a conventional increase in pay, possibly involving the conversion of some existing pay into PRP. It may also be possible to include current profit sharing schemes, provided that the qualifications set out above can be met.

It will not be possible to register schemes with the Inland Revenue until after the 1987 Finance Bill becomes law, which will probably be late July or early August 1987. The Revenue will be issuing full guidance notes then.

Profit sharing scheme

In this plan, the company allocates a percentage of its profits (which need not be fixed) to a trust specially set up for this purpose; this amount is tax deductible to the company. The trustees use the money to acquire shares in the company which they hold in trust for those employees who have agreed to join the scheme.

In due course an employee can ask for the shares to be transferred to him absolutely. Normally no transfer can be made in the first two years; thereafter income tax is chargeable on the original market value of the shares when they are transferred in the third and fourth years and on 75% of that value in the fifth year; thereafter no tax is payable. While the trustees hold the shares, any dividends are paid to the employees entitled to them.

Broadly, the scheme must be open to all full-time employees of the company and the amount that may be allocated to any employee each year is limited to the greater of £1,250 or 10% of his earnings (up to a maximum of £5,000).

SAYE share option scheme

This requires an individual employee to take out a SAYE contract for a period of five years, of the kind described in question 20. At the same time he is granted an option to acquire shares in the company at a set price.

At the end of five or seven years, the employee can cash in the contract and use it to acquire shares in the company at the option price, or he can keep the money and not take up any shares at all.

There are no tax consequences on an individual when he is granted the option nor when he acquires the shares. On any subsequent disposal of the shares he is subject to CGT in the usual way and with the benefit of the normal reliefs (see question 65).

Generally, the scheme must be open to all employees (with a few exceptions). The maximum level of contribution is at present fixed at £100 a month with the minimum normally set at £10 a month; this may be restricted if the employee is already a participant in other SAYE schemes.

Approved share option scheme

This scheme, introduced in 1984, is different to the schemes already described in two major respects.

1 The scheme need only be open to a limited number of employees, selected by the employer, instead of being required to be open to all (or virtually all) employees.

2 The limit on the value of the shares that may be acquired under such a scheme is set at a much higher level than that laid down for either of the other two schemes. The maximum allowed by law is the greater of £100,000 or four times salary, although an individual scheme may provide a lower limit.

There are a number of stringent conditions that need to be satisfied both by the company and by the participants in the scheme; provided that these are met, then any gain arising to the employee on exercising an option which he had been granted is not normally taxable, and only CGT is payable on the disposal of the shares acquired through the scheme.

There is little doubt that this concept has attracted considerable interest, enabling companies to provide selected employees with a major incentive, and a considerable number of schemes have been set up.

61 How can I attract outside investment into my company with the benefit of tax relief?

The *Business Expansion Scheme* (BES) was first introduced in 1981 and substantially modified in 1983. The objective is to encourage private investors to put money into a company and obtain immediate *income tax relief* on that investment. The main features of the scheme are noted below.

1 Income tax relief is given at the individual's highest rate of tax, i.e. perhaps as much as 60%.

2 The maximum amount that may be invested in any one tax year is £40,000. The lower limit is £500 unless the investment is through a BES fund (see point 6 below) when this limit is normally £2,000.

3 Investments may be in any unquoted company trading wholly or mainly in the UK which is engaged in manufacturing, service, construction, retail or wholesale distribution. Certain activities are excluded, particularly those with substantial asset backing or otherwise low exposure to risk.

4 Relief is only on ordinary shares with no special rights which must represent new capital in the company, and these must be held for at least five years. If the shares are disposed of earlier the income tax relief already given is clawed back.

5 The investor must not be connected with the existing shareholders and he may not act as a *paid* director of the company.

6 To enable prospective investors to be linked up with qualifying companies, a number of *BES funds* have been set up. These collect subscriptions from the investors and invest them in suitable companies which the fund managers have investigated. The managers will continue to monitor the progress of the companies on behalf of the investors.

7 As mentioned in point 4, the shares must be held for a minimum of five years. After that the investor may dispose of the shares; where these were issued after 18th March 1986 no CGT is payable on their disposal. For shares issued earlier, CGT is charged only on the excess of the sale proceeds over original cost (i.e. before taking account of any income tax relief).

8 For investments made after 5th April 1987 and made in the first half of the tax year (i.e. between 6th April and 5th October), the investor may carry back half the BES relief to the previous year up to a maximum of £5,000.

As an alternative to BES relief, an individual who invests in the ordinary shares of an unquoted trading company and suffers a loss on their disposal (or on the liquidation of the company) may claim the amount of the loss as a deduction for income tax purposes provided a number of conditions are met (see also question 74).

● **62   When and why is a receiver or liquidator appointed to a company?**

Ever since man first began to trade there have been businesses which have failed, so this is not a new phenomenon, but over recent years there has been a marked increase in the number of bankruptcies and petitions for winding-up, by far the greater number of these being smaller businesses.

If a business fails it is said to be *insolvent* but this is something which is not defined. It is not just a matter of liabilities over assets, so a certain amount of subjective judgement is necessary. It has been said that there appears to be nothing wrong in the fact that directors incur credit, when they know the company is not able to meet all its liabilities as they fall due, but what is most definitely wrong is if the directors continue to incur credit when it is clear the company will *never be able to satisfy its creditors.*

The main areas with regard to corporate failures are *receiverships* and *creditors liquidations;* the latter may be either a voluntary liquidation or a compulsory liquidation. Either way there is normally a formal appointment of a person to take control of the assets and business of the company.

A *receiver* may be appointed by a major creditor, e.g. a bank, to protect the security of its outstanding debt. A receiver, on taking appointment, becomes the agent of the company but this does not suspend the directors of the company, although in practice it will curtail their powers. The appointment will not alter the beneficial ownership by the company itself of its assets or business.

Should the directors prove unable to maintain that the solvency criteria are met, steps must then be taken to commence formal liquidation proceedings. Normally these take the form of a creditors *voluntary winding-up* which involves summoning a meeting of shareholders to pass a winding-up resolution. Not more than one day later a meeting of creditors must be held (called at the same time as the shareholders meeting) and they should confirm the view of insolvency and appoint a liquidator. As an alternative to this, particularly if urgent action is required, the directors of the company may apply to the Court for a *compulsory winding-up order,* which will probably be provisional and subject to a later confirmation. (Proceedings started in this way tend to be more formal and a good deal slower in the long run.) Occasionally, when a liquidation follows a receivership, the assets of a company may be negligible and if the company cannot find an individual willing to act as liquidator (because there is little likelihood of him being paid) the role of the liquidator may be undertaken by the Official Receiver (an officer of the Department of Trade).

It is important to remember that liquidations have different implications to those of receiverships. The latter (i.e. receiverships) can be temporary interruptions in a company's business but the appointment of a liquidator is the forerunner of the dissolution of the company.

Insolvency law has recently been amended and consolidated and a number of changes have been made to various aspects of its operation. In particular, a simplified form of receivership under direction of the Court, known as *administration*, has been introduced and may be appropriate in certain circumstances.

● 63 Are there any special tax considerations relating to groups of companies?

The decision whether to run a business through one company or through a group of companies is dependent upon many factors, not all concerned with taxation, but nevertheless there are taxation aspects to be considered. A company carrying on trading activities is subject to corporation tax, and if those activities are divided up between different companies, even if they are all part of a group, *each company is treated separately, with its own profits and therefore its own corporation tax liability.*

There is no charging of the group as a whole on its total profits, but there is relief which may be claimed in a number of ways:

1 Dividends paid to a parent company may be paid without advance corporation tax (see question 58).

2 Interest and other annual payments may be paid between group companies without deduction of income tax (see question 53).

3 A parent company may pass any surplus advance corporation tax down to a subsidiary which can then use it, subject to certain restrictions, against its own liabilities to corporation tax (see question 58).

4 Certain assets may be transferred within the group without incurring a liability to CGT.

5 All the trades carried on by members of a group are treated as one trade for the purpose of rollover relief for CGT purposes (see question 79).

6 Trading losses and other deductions may be passed to another member of the group by what is called 'group relief'.

There are different rules for each category of relief depending on whether the company is a 51% or 75% subsidiary of its parent; there are also special provisions concerning capital allowances and value added tax (VAT) (see question 99).

It should be noted that none of these arrangements apply to companies which are under the common control of the same individual shareholders without making up a group. In this situation, it may well be worth considering whether there could be advantages in setting up a group structure for these companies.

**64   Can I set up a company overseas and if so what would be the tax   ●
position?**

There is a certain amount of freedom if you should wish to set up a
company overseas; there is no general rule to say that the profits of
an overseas company are to be treated as those of its parent company resident in the UK (as defined in question 52), so this would
seem to give great scope for tax planning. *Beware,* however, of the
stringent 'anti-avoidance' rules which specifically prohibit the transfer of a trade to an overseas (non-resident) company without
obtaining Treasury consent. It is unlawful for any company resident
in the UK to become non-resident without Treasury consent, and
the rules concerning this are very detailed. Consent will be given if a
commercial purpose in transferring the trade or opening a subsidiary
can be shown, plus a net benefit to the UK balance of payments.
Linked with these rules are other provisions which prevent avoidance
of income tax by transactions which result in the transfer of income
to persons who are resident abroad. *There are severe penalties for
failing to comply,* and it is essential to obtain specialist professional
advice if any transactions of this kind are contemplated.

Furthermore, a number of substantial changes have been made,
taking effect from 6th April 1984. These apply in particular to overseas companies controlled by UK residents and operating in low tax
countries (the so-called 'tax havens'). Under these provisions a UK
resident company could be charged to corporation tax on a proportion based on its interest in that company's profits, assets, etc.

Non-resident companies are only liable to pay corporation tax if
they are carrying on a trade through a branch or agency in the UK–
the advantages of transferring the trade overseas as mentioned
above are therefore obvious. If the trade is carried on by a branch
or agency in the UK, the company will pay tax on the branch's
profits, including the following:

1 trading income from the branch;

2 income from property or rights held by the branch;

3 gains accruing from the disposal of assets of the branch or agency
in the UK.

Capital gains realised by a non-resident company may be followed
through to the shareholders. A non-resident company cannot be a
member of a group of companies for UK tax purposes (see question
63).

If a company which is resident in the UK, but trading overseas,
transfers part or all of the trade and assets connected with that trade

to a non-resident company so as to show a capital gain on the transaction, and the consideration received consists partly or wholly of shares and/or loan stock in the company acquiring the trade or asset, the charge to tax on the gain may be postponed. The purpose of this rule is to acknowledge that the gain is primarily a gain on paper only, and gives the company time to acquire the funds to pay the tax; in other words, it is a form of rollover relief (compare question 79). The postponement is subject to certain rules and lasts until the recipient company disposes of some or all of the assets (during six years) or the company which transferred the assets disposes of some or all of the shares it received in return.

In the same way as for individuals (see question 25), where income is taxed in both the UK and overseas, it is usually possible to obtain relief for the overseas direct tax by way of credit against the corresponding UK tax, through the provisions of the appropriate double tax agreement.

5 SOME YOU WIN – SOME YOU LOSE

CAPITAL GAINS TAX AND THE INDIVIDUAL

65   What is CGT? What are the rates of tax and do I still pay CGT if my gains are not substantial?

Capital gains tax (CGT), first introduced on 6th April 1965, is a completely separate tax from income tax. The basis of charge to this tax can be stated as follows: *when a chargeable person disposes of a chargeable asset, either a chargeable gain or an allowable loss will arise.*

You are a *chargeable person* if, during a tax year (i.e. during a year ending on 5th April), you dispose of a *chargeable asset* and at any time during that year you are resident in the UK. There are special rules if you are domiciled outside the UK (see questions 33 and 34); if this is the case you should seek further advice. If you die, all your chargeable assets will be treated as disposed of, but death is *not* an occasion of charge for CGT purposes.

Any form of property, in the widest sense, and whether situated in the UK or not, can be a *chargeable asset.*

In simple terms there is a *chargeable gain* if the proceeds you receive on disposal of an asset exceed the cost of the asset at the date it was acquired. Similarly, if the proceeds on disposal are less than the cost of the asset at acquisition, an *allowable loss* will arise.

This was substantially changed with the introduction, with effect from 6th April 1982 (1st April for companies), of an allowance known as *indexation;* this has been further modified with effect from 6th April 1985 (again 1st April for companies). What follows describes the operation of the relief from the latter dates.

The indexation adjustment applied to the cost of the asset represents the increase in the Retail Prices Index (RPI) from the date that it was acquired to the date of sale so as to reduce the gain or increase the loss. If the asset was acquired before April 1982, the increase in the index is measured from 31st March 1982 and applied to the market value of the asset at that date if this is greater than its cost. These rules are illustrated in these examples:

1 An asset purchased in June 1982 and disposed of in May 1985 will qualify for the indexation allowance applied to the original cost by reference to the increase in the RPI from June 1982 to May 1985.

2 An asset purchased in August 1981 and disposed of in May 1985 will qualify for the indexation allowance applied to the original cost or if greater its market value at 31st March 1982 by reference to the increase in the RPI from that date to May 1985.

For disposals prior to April 1985, the indexation relief was somewhat more limited, the main differences being as follows:

(a) there was a 'waiting period' of 12 months from acquisition before the allowance applied;

(b) for acquisitions prior to April 1982, the allowance applied *only* to original cost;

(c) it was *only* available to reduce or extinguish gains and did not apply to losses at all.

In addition to this relief there is also an annual exemption. If your aggregate chargeable gains do not exceed £6,300 for 1986/87 you will not pay any CGT. Thereafter the amount of the exemption is to be indexed, by the same percentage as the increase in RPI for the December preceding the year of assessment, over the previous December; for 1987/88 the exemption has been fixed at £6,600.

You should therefore consider carefully when making disposals: if you wish to realise a large sum of money by disposing of your assets, by spreading this over two years it is possible there could be a substantial saving of tax. *Remember, you will not pay any CGT if you keep the gains below the specified amount each year.* Refer also to question 74 dealing with losses.

If your chargeable gains *do* exceed the exempt limit you will pay tax at 30% on the excess.

For trusts, the exemption limit is half that for individuals, i.e. £3,150 for 1986/87 and £3,300 for 1987/88; again tax is payable at 30% on the excess. There is no corresponding exemption for companies (see question 57).

● **66 Are any assets exempt from this tax?**

Gains arising on the disposal of certain assets, as set out below, are exempt from CGT; by the same token any loss arising on their disposal is not allowable for these purposes.

Chattels: These are assets which are tangible and moveable. They are exempt if the disposal proceeds are £3,000 or less. (A special computation is necessary if the sum exceeds £3,000.) This does *not* apply to currency (but see under 'Foreign currency' below). There are also special rules dealing with 'sets' of chattels.

Motor cars: These are not chargeable assets unless they are of a type not commonly used as a private vehicle and unsuitable to be so used.

National Savings Certificates, Premium Bonds, etc.: These, and other Government securities which are not transferable, are exempt whenever they are acquired or disposed of. Premium Bond winnings are also exempt.

Government securities ('Gilt-edged'): These are exempt as regards disposals made on or after 2nd July 1986; previously the exemption applied only if the stock had been held for more than 12 months. A similar exemption applies to certain *fixed interest loan stocks* issued after 13th March 1984.

Betting and other winnings: Betting winnings are not chargeable gains and rights to winnings obtained by any pool betting or lottery are not chargeable assets.

Foreign currency: Exempt when disposed of providing it was acquired only for personal and family expenditure.

Medals and decorations: Exempt unless acquired by purchase.

Compensation for damages: Exempt if received for personal or professional wrong or injury; if the damages, etc., relate to an asset, payment will constitute a disposal.

Life assurance policies and deferred annuities: Exempt when disposed of or realised by the original policyholder but *not* when disposed of or realised by another person who acquired them by purchase.

● **67 Is my home a chargeable asset?**

In general, if your dwelling-house is your only or main residence throughout your *period of ownership* there will be no charge to CGT when you sell the property: this exemption extends to the building and (in most cases) up to one acre of land.

However, you may at some time during your period of ownership be required to live elsewhere, through the terms of your employment for instance, or a period of working abroad, in which case your claim that the house is exempt could be affected. The following periods of absence (i.e. the time you are *not living* in your house) do *not* affect your claim, providing you live in the house for a period both before and after (except for points 4 and 5 below) the specified periods of absence.

1 In any circumstances, a period, or periods, not exceeding three years.

2 A period during which you are employed abroad.

3 A period, or periods, not exceeding four years in all during which you are prevented from living in the house by reason of the location of your work, or a condition by your employer requiring you to live elsewhere.

4 The first 12 months of ownership prior to taking up residence during which the house is being built or alterations made.

5 The last two years of ownership are exempt, regardless of whether or not you are living there.

The periods of absence mentioned are also ignored where husband and wife are living together and the conditions are satisfied by the spouse who is not the owner. Where the conditions for exemption from CGT are not satisfied throughout the period of ownership, the gain is apportioned on a time basis to arrive at the amount which is chargeable.

If as a result of a breakdown of marriage, one spouse ceases to occupy the matrimonial home and later transfers it to the other spouse who has continued in occupation, no gain will be chargeable.

Where you are living in 'job-related' accommodation in the circumstances described in question 18, the house which you are buying for your own use may also rank for exemption from CGT as described above.

68   What is my position if I own more than one property?   •

You are only allowed to have one dwelling house at a time for the purposes of the exemption referred to in question 67. If you have more than one house available for your residence at the same time you may choose which one is to be treated as your main residence. A chargeable gain will arise on the disposal of the other property and you should therefore seek advice regarding the value of each– this way it may be that the smaller of the gains arising will be charged to tax by electing for the property giving rise to the larger gain to be exempted as your main residence. Notification of your decision may have effect for up to two years before the date of notice and will continue until varied by further notice. If you do not make a choice the Inspector of Taxes will make it for you: if you disagree with his decision you have the right to appeal (i.e. object) with a view to enabling the matter to be agreed. If you acquire a dwelling house for the sole purpose of selling it again at a profit there will be no exemption from CGT, even though you may live in it for a period.

If the property is used as the residence of a dependent relative of yourself or your spouse and he or she occupies the house rent-free, this property will be exempt from CGT, *in addition* to your own main residence. Relief must be claimed from the Inspector of Taxes and is given in proportion to the part of the period of ownership during which the house is occupied by the relative. Note, this exemption can only apply to *one* dependent relative per marriage (or per claimant, if he or she is single).

There is also an exemption from CGT if you are the owner of a property as the personal representative or trustee of a deceased person. There are certain special rules applicable here and if you consider that this may apply to you, it is advisable to ask for further advice.

69   Does it make any difference if I let my house or take paying guests?   •

You may wish to supplement your income in a tax year by taking a lodger into your home; if he lives with you as part of your family, sharing the living accommodation and taking meals with you, this will *not* affect the exemption for CGT when you sell the property.

If, however, you let part of your home to a paying guest, depending on how much of the home is let (i.e. how many rooms etc.) and for how long, the exemption may be restricted. If you disposed of a house which had been part let *before* 5th April 1980 then there was no relief for that part of the house. If the sale occurred *after* 5th April 1980 there is relief on the let portion of the house but this must not exceed the amount of exemption due on the rest of the house. This relief is only given up to a maximum of £20,000 in any case (limited to £10,000 up to 5th April 1983).

● **70   How am I affected if I use part of my house as an office?**

If you are employed on the basis that you are required to work at home, you may have been advised to claim an income tax allowance for the use of a room in your home as an office (see question 17). Similarly, if you are self-employed you may also have to use part of your home as an office. If part of your house is used *exclusively* for business purposes you may lose the exemption from CGT on that part of the house. You should therefore take care *not* to set aside part of your home exclusively as an office–*be sure that the room you use is also used for other private purposes.*

● **71   Are gifts chargeable to CGT?**

A gift of an asset is a disposal for CGT purposes; however, if you are making a gift there are obviously no safe proceeds, so the chargeable gain is computed by substituting (for sale proceeds) the *market value of the gift* at the date it was given. For these purposes the market value is the price which the asset might reasonably be expected to fetch if it were sold on the open market.

There are certain gifts which are altogether exempt from CGT:
1 transfers between married persons living together;
2 gifts of cash in sterling;
3 gifts to charities;
4 gifts of land, buildings and chattels to the National Trust and other similar bodies, and of works of art etc. for the national benefit.

● **72   If I make a gift which is not exempt from CGT, is there any relief that I can claim?**

If the gift is not exempt, the chargeable gain will be assessed and the person making the gift (i.e. the donor) would normally pay the CGT due. From 6th April 1980 if the gift is made to an individual resident in the UK the gain can be *held over*. This means that instead of the *donor* paying the tax, the gain will be deducted from the acquisition value of the gift; this in turn means that the *donee* (i.e. the person receiving the gift) will pay the CGT (subject to any exemptions that he may be able to claim) when the asset is eventually sold, as he has a *lower* acquisition value to be deducted from the sale proceeds, leaving a *higher* chargeable gain. Both the donee and the donor must elect jointly for this relief to apply.

Beware, however, if the donee becomes non-resident in the UK within six years of the end of the tax year in which the gift was made and he still has the asset: the 'heldover' liability becomes immediately payable. Furthermore, if they cannot get it from the donee, the Inland Revenue has power to tax the donor.

This holdover relief is also available for gifts made to a trust, and for assets transferred out of a trust, for example to a beneficiary.

A useful point to remember (although perhaps rather macabre) is that death is not an occasion of charge for CGT purposes, so that if an asset is given to a donee who subsequently dies, if both parties signed an election for this holdover relief to apply there will be no CGT to pay on that gift. Note, if although it is a gift the donor actually receives consideration from the donee in respect of the gift, there may be some CGT to pay.

73 Can I save tax by claiming expenses?

If you incur expenditure when acquiring or disposing of an asset this can be used to reduce the chargeable gain. Expenses which are allowable fall into the following categories.

1 Costs incidental to the acquisition: These may only be deducted if they are actually incurred by the person acquiring the asset. They must be incurred *wholly and exclusively* for the purpose of the acquisition; this would apply to fees, commission, cost of transfer, etc., together with advertising costs incurred in finding a seller.

2 Improvements: Again, the expenditure must be incurred *wholly and exclusively* in respect of the asset, this time to enhance its value. Such expenditure *must* be reflected in the state or nature of the asset at the time of its disposal.

3 Establishing rights to the asset: Expenditure is allowable if it is incurred *wholly and exclusively* for the purposes of establishing, preserving or defending your title to the asset. This is a very strict rule and operates narrowly.

4 Costs incidental to the disposal: These are defined in the same way as the costs of acquisition and cover legal fees and the cost of advertising to find a buyer. Costs reasonably incurred in making or finding a valuation for CGT purposes will also be allowed.

General investment advice and expenditure on financial journals are *not* allowable.

● **74   If I make a capital loss, can I turn this to my advantage?**

You will no doubt have realised by now that it is to your advantage to keep your chargeable gains below the exemption limit mentioned in question 65. The treatment of losses incurred in both the current and previous years can play an important part in reducing your chargeable gains to this figure.

Losses realised in the current year must be set off against gains for the current year as far as it is possible to do so and any excess may then be carried forward. However, *losses brought forward* from a previous year need only be set off against current year gains to the extent necessary to reduce those gains to the exemption limit. The benefit of this is two-fold, as you are still able to carry any excess losses forward but you have also been able to utilise the tax-free exemption limit.

Losses brought forward from previous years are therefore of importance, and if you are approaching the end of a tax year with no realised gains it may be possible to create losses by *bed and breakfast* transactions (see question 75) to build up a bank of losses to carry forward to future years. *A word of warning:* if you have already realised gains in the current year, 'bed and breakfast' transactions to create losses should only be carried out in order to remove the gains from the taxable threshold, as any current year losses which reduce the gains to below the exemption level will be wasted.

As a general rule you cannot set your capital losses against your other income and if you are in business you cannot set trading losses against capital gains. However, it is possible to claim the set-off of a loss arising on the disposal of shares in an *unquoted* trading company against your other income for income tax purposes *provided* that the shares were acquired by subscription in cash or money's worth and not bought from a previous shareholder. The shares must *never* have been quoted on The Stock Exchange and there are other tests to be satisfied before the relief is given.

Another general rule concerning losses is that they may not be carried back to be set against gains of an earlier year; there is an exception to this in the year of death when losses can be carried back for three years, covering the later gains first.

If you make a disposal of an asset to a *connected person* and incur a loss, that loss may only be utilised against gains arising from future disposals to the same person, if he or she is still connected with you. As an individual you are 'connected' with any relative of yourself or your spouse and the spouse of any of those relatives. If you are a trustee you are 'connected' with the settlor and any other person or body corporate connected with the settlement. Finally, if you are in partnership you are 'connected' with each partner and their respective spouses and relatives.

There is also loss relief in respect of a *qualifying loan*–see question 79.

75   What is a bed and breakfast transaction?

Generally, *bed and breakfast* transactions relate to quoted stocks and shares, i.e. those dealt in on The Stock Exchange. If such shares are sold on one day and repurchased through The Stock Exchange on the following day, then, provided that the sale and repurchase takes place within the same Stock Exchange 'account', there can be an opportunity for saving some of the incidental costs of the deal, in particular the stockbroker's charges and stamp duty on the transfer documents.

Prior to the introduction of *indexation* for CGT purposes (see question 65), this arrangement provided a means of crystallising an accrued loss on a holding of quoted shares where their quoted prices had fallen by comparison with the price at which they had been purchased originally. This could then be used as an allowable loss to be set against other gains (see question 74).

However, as part of the changes following the bringing in of indexation with effect from April 1982, special rules were laid down dealing with the identification of purchases and sales of investments within the same Stock Exchange account; these had the effect of making transactions of this kind less attractive than had previously been the case. However, with the further changes introduced in April 1985 (see question 65), the earlier rules were restored and bed and breakfast transactions can again be used to advantage as a means of mitigating CGT liabilities.

76 If I am married, how does this affect my capital gains position?

The rules concerning husband and wife are as follows.

1 Transfers of assets between spouses who are living together are regarded as made on a basis of *no gain, no loss*. (The exceptions to this are on death or the transfer of trading stock to or from either spouse.)

2 The houses of husband and wife living together are dealt with in questions 67 and 68.

3 Capital gains and losses are calculated for each spouse separately; unrelieved losses of one are to be set against net gains of the other except where there is an election to the contrary, which must be made before 6th July in the year following the end of the year of assessment.

4 The net gains and losses are assessed jointly on the husband, except for the year of marriage when the wife is assessed as if she is a single person (unless the marriage took place on 6th April). If the tax remains unpaid by the husband the Inland Revenue may press for payment by the wife, up to the amount she would have to pay if a separate assessment election was in force (see point 5 below).

5 Either party to the marriage may claim for separate assessment for CGT if they make application before 6th July in the year following the end of the year of assessment. There is the same time limit for revoking such an election. The total payable is to remain unchanged but the wife will have an assessment on her own gains and she will therefore be liable to pay her own tax.

6 The annual exemption from CGT applies as if it is divided between the spouses living together, in proportion to their respective taxable amounts, or where these amounts total less than the exempt amount and there are losses brought forward from previous years, in such proportions as they agree.

There is only limited scope therefore for saving tax as a husband and wife team for CGT purposes. The advantages are that the exemption may be split between you in whatever proportion you choose. This can in certain circumstances preserve the losses of one spouse, to be carried forward, although against this, the other spouse may pay more tax in the current year.

Children who are minors are entitled to their own exemption limits which gives scope for future reduction in a family's CGT burden if transfers of part of a family shareholding are made to the children at any early stage–if this should create a loss, refer to the rules on 'connected persons', covered in question 74. It is essential that any such transfers to the children be clearly and indisputably for their benefit.

77   I have assets which I acquired before CGT was introduced on 6th April 1965. What is the position on these?

CGT was not introduced until 6th April 1965 and it follows that you should *not* be taxed on any gain arising *before* that date. There are two answers to this question depending on whether assets are quoted shares and securities, or unquoted shares or property. The rules governing each category are as follows:

Quoted shares and securities: Two computations of the gain/loss are necessary when the shares are sold. The first is of the difference between the selling price and the original cost of the shares, the second is of the difference between the selling price and the market value of the shares, as quoted on The Stock Exchange, on 6th April 1965: the smaller gain or loss is accepted when the computations are compared. If one computation shows a gain and the other a loss the disposal is treated as a 'no gain–no loss' situation.

These rules also apply to land held on 6th April 1965 which is subsequently disposed of at a price including development value.

Other assets including unquoted shares and land without development value: Here the gain/loss is calculated on a 'time apportionment basis' (with certain exceptions), to and from 6th April 1965. The computation is the sale proceeds less the acquisition cost which gives an overall gain deemed to have arisen evenly over the period of ownership. The gain is then apportioned to and from 6th April 1965 and only the latter part is charged to tax after any relief for inflation (see question 65) or other exemptions. (If the asset was acquired before 6th April 1945 the gain is only calculated from the 1945 date but still using the original cost.)

As an alternative, it is permitted to make an election for the market value at 6th April 1965 to be used in place of the original cost, in which case there is no time-apportionment (the gain is sale proceeds less market value). The election is *irrevocable* and *must* be made within two years of the end of the year of assessment in which the disposal is made. Unfortunately, the Revenue will not discuss a valuation until an election has been made, which could mean you end up paying tax on a higher figure than if time-apportionment was used–and there is then nothing you can do.

It is important to refer all matters concerning such assets held on 6th April 1965 to a professional adviser who will be able to advise whether or not an election for the 6th April 1965 value would appear to be to your advantage.

● **78 What are paper for paper transactions and how do they affect my capital gains position?**

If you hold shares in a public company you may have realised that some transactions do not involve the actual buying and selling of shares. For instance, the company may decide not to distribute its profits as dividends, but to capitalise part of them (perhaps to build up reserves), in which case there may be a *bonus issue* of additional shares to the existing shareholders for which they pay nothing. On the other hand, a company seeking to increase its capital by an issue of new shares may allocate some of the new shares at a preferential price to its existing shareholders. This is referred to as a *rights issue*. In the *reorganisation of a company's capital,* blocks of shares may be exchanged or two companies may *amalgamate* or *merge* (or one company may *take over* another) by the exchange of share capital. In none of these situations are you buying shares for cash in the normal way.

For the purposes of CGT, if you acquire shares through any of the above circumstances, this is not classed as a chargeable occasion. The new or increased holding is, on the occasion of a later disposal, treated as having been acquired at the same time and at the same cost (plus any payments made for 'rights' issues) as the original holding.

In some instances you will be given the new shares automatically (e.g. 'bonus' issue), but with a 'rights' issues you are able to make a choice as to whether or not you take up the new shares. If you decide not to take up the offer you may then 'sell the rights' to the new shares for a (usually) relatively small consideration. This is a chargeable occasion, but if the amount you receive does not exceed 5% of the market value (on that day) of the shares you already hold there will be no charge to CGT at that time. The amount received is deducted from the acquisition cost of the holding, thus increasing the gain on an eventual disposal.

If the transaction offered by a company means you receive a capital distribution in money or money's worth (possibly in addition to the shares offered) which is not treated as income, you are then treated as having disposed of a part interest in the shares you hold and a gain is then calculated using only a proportion of the acquisition cost as the base cost for this purpose.

79 Are there any other reliefs for which I may qualify in certain circumstances?

The following few brief notes concerning other reliefs are not a comprehensive guide. The rules are complicated and if you consider that you may qualify for relief under any of these headings you *must* seek further advice.

Rollover relief: A trader disposing of assets used exclusively for the purposes of his trade, *who applies the sale proceeds in purchasing other assets to be used for a trade,* may elect to defer CGT by deducting the amount of the chargeable gain arising on the sale of the old asset from the acquisition cost of the new asset. The purchase of the new asset must take place within one year before, or three years after, the disposal of the old asset, but these time limits may be extended at the Revenue's discretion.

If only part of the sale proceeds is used to purchase the new asset there is a corresponding loss of relief. Furthermore, this relief is only given on any gain remaining when *retirement relief* (see below) has been taken into account.

Retirement relief: This relief applies where the individual is over 60 years of age (or has to retire earlier through ill-health) and disposes of whole or part of a business which is owned by him or of shares and securities in his 'family' company. There are many conditions to be satisfied relating to the transaction and past history of the business or family company concerned, if these are fulfilled throughout a maximum qualifying period of ten years, relief will be given to its full extent. For periods of less than ten years a proportionate reduction is made, on a time basis, so that the minimum 'relevant percentage' is 10%, based on a minimum period of one year. Furthermore, relief is given if, in association with a sale of shares in his family company, the individual also disposes of an asset owned by himself that has been used by the company–again, there are various conditions to be fulfilled.

The maximum relief is £125,000 for disposals taking place on or after 6th April 1987; prior to that date the limit was £100,000. The relief is given against the part of the gain relating to *chargeable business assets*.

Qualifying loan loss relief: First of all, it must be established what constitutes a *qualifying loan*.

The loan must have been given, after 11th April 1978, to a resident of the UK for use wholly in his trade (so that the borrower may also be a company), profession or vocation. The provisions do not apply to borrowings in the form of loan stock or any other similar marketable security; losses on these may be claimed in the normal way.

Provided that the Inspector of Taxes is satisfied that the claimant and the borrower were not spouses living together (or companies in the same group) and that the lender has not assigned his right of recovery, loss relief may be allowed to the extent that part of the capital element of the loan has become irrecoverable. If at a later date following a loss claim, all or part of the sum is recovered, a chargeable gain will arise on the claimant.

● 80   **When do I pay my CGT and are there any other administrative details I should know?**

CGT becomes due and payable on *1st December following the end of the year of assessment* to which the gains relate, or 30 days after the issue of the notice of assessment, whichever is later. It is therefore possible to make a disposal on 6th April 1987 (or later) on which the CGT will not be due until 1st December 1988 at the earliest.

If you disagree with the assessment you have the same right to appeal as for income tax and the same provisions also apply to a request for postponement of part of the tax charged, interest on unpaid tax and payment of a supplement on tax repayments (see question 3).

Where the consideration to be paid in respect of an asset you have sold is paid to you by instalments, it is possible for you to *pay tax by instalments* over a period not exceeding eight years, if you can satisfy the Revenue that to pay all the tax in one sum would cause you hardship.

Finally, do not think that if the Revenue does not know of the gains you have made you will not have to pay the tax; the Revenue has its own way of tracing property transactions and share dealings. You should notify the Revenue of your gains when you complete your income tax return and there are *penalties for failure to do so*– see question 4.

6 CAPITAL WAYS OF SAVING TAX

INHERITANCE TAX

81   What is inheritance tax (IHT)? What are the rates of tax? ●

Assets passing at death have been subject to various forms of taxation since *estate duty* was introduced in 1894. Estate duty only taxed assets passing on death and certain lifetime gifts, but CGT also applied on death occurring between 1965 and 1971.

In 1974 *capital transfer tax* was introduced as a wide ranging tax on gifts made during lifetime and on assets passing on death on a cumulative basis. Special provisions were also brought in to tax various forms of trust.

Following the Budget speech of 18th March 1986, a number of radical changes were introduced to the existing scheme, including a change of name to *inheritance tax* (IHT). The new scheme, which came into operation on that date, applies generally to assets passing on *death* and to *gifts made within seven years before death*. Certain other categories of lifetime gifts may also be subject to the tax and these are considered in questions 82 and 83.

The rates of tax applicable to transfers made on or after 17th March 1987 are as follows.

Portion of value		Rate of tax
Lower limit £	Upper limit £	%
Nil	90,000	Nil
90,000	140,000	30
140,000	220,000	40
220,000	330,000	50
330,000	–	60

These rate bands are to be adjusted annually in line with changes in the RPI.

Gifts made up to seven years before the death are included with assets passing upon death at their value at the date of the gift, but using the rates of tax in force at the date of death. However, only gifts made up to *three years* before the death will be included in full; for gifts made earlier, a form of tapering relief will be available so that only a proportion of the full charge will apply. The table below shows the relevant details.

Yours between gift and death	Proportion of full charge %
3-4	80
4-5	60
5-6	40
6-7	20

● **82   Are any lifetime gifts affected by IHT?**

In general, for gifts made on or after 18th March 1986 other than those made within seven years before the death of the donor, there will be no lifetime charge to tax:
1 on gifts between individuals;
2 on gifts into accumulation and maintenance trusts (see question 93) or into trusts for the disabled;
3 on gifts made into interest in possession trusts (i.e. those where an individual has an entitlement to income) on or after 17th March 1987.

However, a charge will be made on gifts into other forms of trust made at any time. The rates applicable will be half those that would be applicable using the table in question 81.

● **83   Are certain types of gift subject to special treatment?**

So far we have assumed that a 'gift' is what it says it is, namely a free and unencumbered transfer of an asset.

However, special rules apply where the gift is not made outright: technically this is referred to as a *gift with reservation* and would apply where the donor continues to enjoy some benefit from the gifted asset. A simple example of this would be where an individual gives his house to another member of the family, subject to him (the donor) having the right to go on living in it rent-free. In such a case, the gift would be treated as made only when the reservation is released or the enjoyment finally ceases. In the example of the house already mentioned, this could apply when the donor moved out to live elsewhere giving up his rights of occupation, or perhaps on his death. If the gift is thereby treated as taking place on the donor's death or within a period of seven years before, IHT will apply as described in question 81.

84 How are husband and wife treated for IHT?

Unlike income tax and CGT, husband and wife are treated as separate individuals for IHT purposes.

Furthermore, a transfer between husband and wife is generally exempt from the tax, with one exception. Where the spouse receiving the gift is domiciled outside the UK (see question 85), only the first £55,000 will be exempt; any balance may therefore come within the 'seven year' charge (see question 81).

Where one spouse has substantial assets and the other has not, it may be worthwhile reducing the possible exposure to tax on death by topping up the smaller estate so that each can obtain the benefit of the lower rates of tax.

85 How is IHT affected by my domicile?

If you are *domiciled* in the UK (see question 33) you will be liable to pay IHT on all your assets irrespective of where they are situated. If you are domiciled abroad tax is still payable, but only on any assets you have situated in the UK. The meaning of domicile is discussed in general terms in questions 33 and 34 but this is modified for IHT purposes. In many situations *it is possible to be caught for IHT even if for other purposes it is accepted that you have abandoned or never adopted a UK domicile.*

86 When is the tax payable and who is responsible for paying it?

Tax is due within six months of the end of the month in which the death occurred, and interest at 8% runs from that date. Different rules apply in relation to those lifetime gifts which are chargeable to tax.

The persons primarily responsible for paying the tax are the *personal representatives,* but the Inland Revenue do have power to follow the liability through to any person in whom the property passing is vested after death. In the case of a lifetime gift which is caught, the tax attributable to that gift is normally collectible from the recipient unless there is a special provision in the donor's will allowing it to be charged against his estate.

Where any tax has already been paid on a gift, for example under the previous rules applicable to capital transfer tax, this will be allowed as a credit against the corresponding tax arising on the death.

● **87   What are the alternatives if I do not have the necessary funds available to pay the tax?**

If the necessary funds to pay the tax are not available, the Revenue may accept any of the following property as a payment in kind: land; buildings and contents associated with those buildings; pictures, prints, books, manuscripts, works of art, scientific objects or other items, or collections of such items, should they be of national, scientific, historic or artistic interest.

● **88   Can I make gifts which are not chargeable to IHT?**

There are certain categories of *lifetime transfers* which are not chargeable to tax; these reliefs do not apply on death.

Annual exemption: The first £3,000 of transfers each tax year is exempt; any unused relief may be carried forward for one year only against transfers in excess of the limit for the following year. Unless there is a regular pattern of making gifts, so that these take place at least every other year, some of the benefit of this exemption may be lost.

'Small' gifts: The first £250 of transfers to any one individual in each tax year is exempt in addition to the annual exemption mentioned above. Unused relief cannot be used in a later year. The exemption applies only to outright gifts, not to settlements. It is therefore possible to pay any number of people £250 in a year and still be outside the scope of IHT altogether. However, the relief cannot be used to cover the first slice of a larger gift; thus a transfer of £1,000 could be covered by the annual exemption, leaving £2,000, but not covered by the £250 small gifts exemption so as use only £750 of the annual exemption.

Marriage gifts: Transfers made in consideration of marriage are exempt, but only within set limits which vary according to the degree of affinity between the transferor and the parties to the marriage. If the transferor is a parent of one of the parties to the marriage, he may give £5,000; if the transferor is a more remote ancestor he may give £2,500; if the transferor is one of the parties to the marriage the limit is £2,500; anyone else may give £1,000.

For this exemption it is important to ensure that there is evidence that the gift is actually made in consideration of the marriage. The gift should be completed *before* the marriage; unless special steps are taken, such a gift cannot normally be made after the marriage.

Normal expenditure out of income: If a transfer is effected out of income it may not be relevant to IHT. To qualify for this exemption, the Revenue must be satisfied as to the following three conditions:
1 The transfer is made as part of the normal expenditure of the transferor.
2 The transfer is made out of his income (comparing one year with another).
3 After allowing for all such transfers the transferor is left with sufficient income to maintain his usual standard of living.

The expenditure must be 'habitual' and the Revenue will look for a pattern of payments made to the same person. The expenditure must involve cash outlay; gifts of assets will only qualify if they were bought for the purposes of making the gift. 'Income' is taken as net of income tax for these purposes.

The following transfers are exempt from tax both as lifetime gifts and on death.

Charities: Transfers to charities, whether during the donor's lifetime or by his will on his death, are wholly exempt from IHT.

Political parties: If you should wish to make a donation to a qualifying political party, this will be exempt from IHT as a lifetime transfer. But transfers in excess of £100,000 made on death or within 12 months prior to death are taxable.

A political party only 'qualifies' if it has two MPs or if it has one MP and gained at least 150,000 votes at the last General Election.

National heritage

There are three different exemptions in this category, viz. gifts for national purposes, gifts for public benefit and conditional exemption.

It is essential that specialist professional advice is taken in connection with any possible claim for relief under these provisions.

1 Gifts for national purposes: The transfer is exempt if it becomes the property of specified bodies–certain museums, galleries, and trust funds are specified by name (e.g. National Trust); similar national institutions may be approved by the Treasury; many museums and art galleries maintained by local authorities and Government departments are also included.

2 Gifts for public benefit: The transfer is exempt if it is property which then becomes the property of a non-profit making organisation, provided the Treasury gives its consent. The property so transferred may be land, buildings, works of art, etc., and the Treasury will be looking for items of outstanding scenic, historic, scientific, architectural or aesthetic value, as appropriate. The Treasury usually require undertakings to be given to preserve the asset and to provide reasonable access to the public.

3 Conditional exemption: The property involved in this relief is basically the same as for gifts for the public benefit (see point 2 above). The transfer is conditionally exempt to the extent that it is attributable to property designated by the Treasury. The property remains in private ownership and the Treasury will require various undertakings to be given before the exemption is allowed. IHT becomes payable if there is a breach in the conditions or if the property is sold, unless the undertakings are renewed.

● **89   What is excluded property?**

Excluded property is not included in an individual's estate either for the purpose of lifetime transfers or in the event of his death.

Excluded property includes the following:

1 Property situated outside the UK if the beneficial owner is domiciled abroad (see questions 33, 34 and 85).

2 A reversionary interest (i.e. something which reverts to you) providing it was *not* purchased by you.

3 Certain Government securities beneficially owned by persons not domiciled or habitually resident in the UK (see questions 33, 34 and 85).

4 National Savings owned by persons domiciled in the Channel Islands or Isle of Man.

5 Property passing as a result of death on active service.

6 Cash options under approved annuity schemes.

7 Overseas pensions.

8 Property owned by members of visiting armed forces.

It should be particularly noted that an individual's private residence is *not* excluded from the charge to IHT so that there is no exemption corresponding to that applicable for CGT (see questions 67 and 68).

**90   If I have made transfers chargeable to IHT, are there any reliefs I   ●
can claim?**

The following gives a few brief notes with regard to reliefs which may be available if you have transferred a particular form of property, or the circumstances are unusual. This is *not* a comprehensive guide and if you consider you may be eligible for any of the following you should seek further specialist advice.

Business property relief: Basically this relief provides that if you transfer 'relevant business property' the value transferred will be reduced by a percentage which will vary depending on the type of business property concerned. The relief can be claimed whether the transfer is made during your lifetime or at death, and there is no limit to the value transferred which can qualify for this relief. Relevant business property includes:

– a business or interest in a business (reduction 50%);

– shares/securities in a company which was controlled by the transferor immediately before the transfer (reduction 50%);

– non-controlling shareholdings of more than 25% in a company where the shares are not quoted on a recognised stock exchange or the Unlisted Securities Market (reduction 50%) (this relief only applies to transfers made on or after 17th March 1987);

– other non-controlling shareholdings in a company not quoted on a recognised stock exchange or the Unlisted Securities Market (reduction 30%);

– in certain circumstances, land, buildings, machinery and plant used for business purposes (reduction 30%).

There are many conditions to be satisfied before the property is eligible for relief.

Agricultural property relief: This relief applies to transfers made during your lifetime or at death and provides that if the value transferred is attributable to the agricultural value of agricultural property in the UK, and the property is owned by a working farmer, the *value may be reduced by 50% of the agricultural value.*

Where the land is let to a working farmer, for transfers made after 15th March 1983, the landlord may claim a reduction of 30% of the agricultural value.

This relief is subject to various tests as to ownership and occupation on death and where relevant on transfer within seven years before death.

Relief for woodlands: A claim can be made that the value of trees or underwood growing on land in the UK (which is not agricultural property) be left out of account in determining the value transferred on the owner's death. Relief is to be claimed, by the person who would be liable to pay the tax, within two years following the death, but this time limit may be extended. The basic condition to be satisfied is that the woodlands must have been owned by the deceased for five years prior to his death or have been acquired by gift or inheritance. There will be no charge to tax unless the woodlands are disposed of either by sale or gift so it is possible to extend the relief through a succession of deaths.

Voidable transfer: Inheritance tax is repayable in respect of any transfer which is subsequently declared void by an enactment or rule of law, e.g. bankruptcy.

● **91   How is my estate valued at my death?**

Your *estate at death* includes all the property of whatever description to which you were beneficially entitled. An exception to this is life assurance policies which are included in the estate at their full value. At death your estate will generally also include all property contained in a settlement if you had a vested interest in the capital or income of it.

For many forms of property, the value will be an obvious amount, or relatively easy to calculate, but problems occur when valuing *unquoted shares* because a hypothetical situation must be used–this involves a hypothetical sale in a hypothetical open market between a vendor and purchaser both of whom are also hypothetical! This principle for valuing unquoted shares has been built up over many years, and it is now well established that the larger the holding, in general the greater the price that it should command. In certain circumstances adjustments may be made to the open market value in arriving at the amounts for IHT and CGT purposes, so that there may be material differences between the valuations applied to the two taxes.

Shares beneficially owned by either husband or wife, or any trust in which either spouse has a vested interest in the income or capital, or any charity as the result of a gift made by either spouse after 15th April 1976, are *related property* for IHT (but not CGT) purposes. Any *related property is then treated as a single holding* for valuing any transfer made by the husband or wife. It follows therefore that although the separate shareholdings of husband or wife may only be minority holdings, when taken together they may constitute a majority holding, and it is as part of the latter that the IHT valuation must be considered.

92 Is it possible to change arrangements made by a will after death has taken place, and if so, what are the tax consequences?

It is possible to change arrangements made by a will by what is called a *deed of family arrangement* which effectively permits a deceased person's will to be re-written after his death and any tax will then be calculated as if the original will had been written in the same terms as the deed. For IHT and CGT purposes the charge is effective from the date of death, but for income tax purposes it is only effective from the date of the deed.

The deed must be entered into within two years of death, by an instrument in writing, and the persons doing so must notify the Inland Revenue within six months. The point of making such a deed would seem to be lost if additional tax became payable, but if this is the case (perhaps because the new arrangements have been set up for other than tax reasons), the persons liable to pay the additional liability (i.e. primarily the personal representatives) must be included with the persons joining in the agreement.

All persons who may benefit under the original will must agree to the making of a deed of family arrangement if it affects their interests. This may not be feasible where the interests, even quite remote, of infant beneficiaries are involved. It is essential to obtain expert legal advice on the possibility of entering into such arrangements.

● **93   Are there any special provisions relating to settlements?**

The use of settlements as a form of tax planning has always attracted considerable attention from the legislators, and settlements of all kinds are specially treated for IHT purposes. This is a highly complex area and what follows is only a brief summary of the current position.

Apart from the trusts mentioned in question 82, and except for certain special forms of trust described below, tax is charged at half the normal rate on any gifts made into settlement at any time.

Where the trust has an *interest in possession* (broadly there is a person entitled to receive the income of the trust), the assets of the trust will be treated as if they were part of that person's estate for the purpose of determining the tax payable on his death.

Where the trust is what is called *discretionary*, so that there is no one entitled to any part of the income or capital of the trust, a special charge to tax at reduced rates is levied on the assets of the trust every ten years or when any assets are transferred out, for example to a beneficiary.

Special treatment is given to the following types of settlement.

Accumulation and maintenance trust: The following conditions *must* be met:
1 One or more persons will become entitled to an interest in possession (which may be absolute or need only be an interest in the income) on or before attaining the age of 25.
2 Income is accumulated unless used for the maintenance, education or benefit of a beneficiary.
3 Not more than 25 years have elapsed since the creation of the settlement, *or* all beneficiaries are grandchildren of a common grandparent.

If the trust qualifies, no tax will arise on gifts made into it more than seven years before the settlor's death, the periodic charge mentioned above for discretionary trusts will not be payable and no further tax will arise when a beneficiary attains his interest.

Protective trust: This would come into force in the instance where the principal beneficiary attempts to assign his interest to someone else. This would give the trustees discretion over the income but the periodic charge already referred to would not be payable even on the subsequent death of the principal beneficiary.

Trust for the mentally disabled: There is no tax payable if the trust is created for a mentally disabled person more than seven years before the donor's death and the periodic charge is deferred until the death of the mentally handicapped person.

Charitable trust: Trusts which are wholly charitable are not subject to a tax on entry and they are exempt from the periodic charge and from tax on all distributions.

Employee trust: A trust of this type may qualify for deferment of tax where the beneficiaries are restricted to persons of a class defined by reference to employment, persons married to those so defined, or charities. Payments to beneficiaries are not classed as a capital distribution and the periodic charge is deferred until a capital distribution payment is made.

7 THE INDIRECT TAX YOU MUST PAY

VALUE ADDED TAX

94 How does value added tax (VAT) operate in relation to my business?

VAT is a wide ranging form of indirect tax which has an impact on most forms of business operation in the UK. Currently the tax applies to *all* supplies of goods and services made in the course of a business with certain exceptions which are considered in question 97. The tax is presently charged at a single rate of 15%.

A *taxable person* (see question 95) is required to charge tax (known as *output tax*) on all supplies (with certain exceptions, see question 97) made by him to his customers and account for this tax, normally on a quarterly basis, to HM Customs and Excise (C & E) for it. Against this liability, the taxable person is entitled to take credit, subject to certain restrictions, for tax on supplies of goods and services made to him *for business purposes* (known as *input tax*) during the same accounting period (but see question 98).

Normally, output tax has to be included in a trader's VAT return on the basis of invoices *issued*, not necessarily paid for. Similarly, input tax is claimed on the basis of invoices *received*. However, the Chancellor of the Exchequer announced proposals in his Budget speech on 17th March 1987 which could allow traders having a turnover of less than £250,000 a year to elect to go onto a cash accounting basis. This means that these businesses would only have to account to C & E for VAT when it had actually *collected* the tax from its customers; it would thereby get automatic relief for bad debts which is otherwise only available in very limited circumstances. By the same token, input tax could only be claimed as the bills were actually paid. It is intended to make this relief available in October 1987.

In 1988 it is planned to bring in an arrangement whereby traders having a turnover of less than £250,000 a year can opt to make their VAT returns once a year instead of quarterly. The trader would be

127

required to make nine monthly payments on an estimated basis during the year concerned and pay the balance with his return.

Where a trader suffers more input tax in a period than the output tax he has to account for, C & E will repay the excess. However, where a business does not make any taxable supplies, either because its turnover is not sufficient for it to be registered for VAT (see question 95) or because all its supplies are *exempt* from VAT (see question 97), it is not entitled to any credit for input tax, as described above. If a business has a mixture of taxable and exempt supplies, as defined for VAT purposes, some restriction may be applied to the amount of input tax for which it can claim credit. This is looked at further in question 98.

● 95   When do I have to register for VAT?

One of the most important features of VAT is registration: VAT is to be accounted for by *taxable persons* who make *taxable supplies* of goods and services in the UK, during the course or furtherance of their business. A *taxable person* is someone who makes or intends to make taxable supplies while he is registered or required to be registered. The point at which you are liable to be registered is governed by various turnover limits, but if you are an 'intending trader' or your turnover is below these levels, you may register voluntarily, at the discretion of C & E.

If you have just started in business the date or point at which you should register is clearly important. Output tax can be an unexpected expense but perhaps even more important, if you are not registered for VAT purposes, you cannot reclaim the input tax you have paid on goods and services supplied to you; this could be most important in the earliest days of your business before you are obliged to register for VAT purposes, although under certain circumstances it may be possible to reclaim tax on goods or services supplied prior to registration. The limits of turnover should be kept under review: these are currently £7,250 at the end of a quarter and £21,300 over a whole year.

If, at the end of a quarter, your turnover exceeds the limit, you will be required to register unless it is agreed that the annual limit will not be exceeded; tax will then be chargeable from the 21st day following the end of that quarter. Failure to get this right can result in a great deal of unnecessary expense–if at any time C & E think the annual limit might be reached you will be ordered to register immediately and tax may be assessed from an earlier date.

Remember that the onus is on you as the trader to notify C & E that you should be registered for VAT.

You should also be aware that stringent powers of enforcement have recently been given to C & E in connection with VAT, particularly in relation to the timely and accurate completion of VAT returns. Penalties for failure to comply with these new requirements could be substantial.

These powers are being introduced in stages, but it is vital that traders who are involved in VAT should review and if appropriate overhaul their accounting arrangements to ensure that they can meet these requirements without penalty.

96 If I am registered for VAT, what happens if there is a change in my circumstances? ●

After you have registered for VAT purposes, if there is any change in your circumstances you *must* inform your local VAT office and there are penalties for failure to do so. Many of the possible changes which could occur will require the *deregistration* of your business, which must be notified to the VAT office within ten days of the change. The most important circumstances are as follows:

1 The business is closed down or sold.

2 The proprietor of the business takes one or more persons into partnership.

3 A partnership ceases to exist but one of the former partners becomes the sole proprietor of the business.

4 A company is incorporated to take over a business previously carried on by a sole proprietor or partnership.

5 A business previously carried on by a company is taken over by a sole proprietor or partnership.

6 Taxable supplies cease for some other reason.

A business may apply to deregister for VAT purposes if its annual turnover is expected to fall below £19,500. From 1st June 1987, the limit for deregistration is raised to £20,300.

When your registration is cancelled you may be awaiting either tax invoices for services already provided to you or the completion of services relating to the business you carried on when you were registered. If so, you may not be able to claim input tax on these services on your final VAT return, but you may be able to claim a special repayment subsequently.

Other changes in circumstances may be dealt with by a simple amendment to your registration (e.g. address, change in the trading name of the business, etc.).

● 97 What exceptions are there to VAT's standard rate charge?

For a variety of social and political reasons, each country that operates a VAT system deems it appropriate that certain supplies should not be subject to VAT. The UK is no exception to this procedure and indeed it has probably the widest range of exclusions from VAT of any country in Europe.

Exclusions from the charge to VAT operate in two ways: zero rating and exemption.

Zero rating

In this case, the supplier concerned is treated as being subject to VAT at a nil rate, but otherwise regarded as being taxable. There is therefore no effect on the trader's entitlement to reclaim input tax (see question 94).

The more important zero rated supplies are as follows:
– exports of goods;
– food excluding restaurant meals and catering supplies;
– books, newspapers and other publications;
– fuel and power;
– construction or demolition of buildings;
– alteration or substantial reconstruction of listed buildings;
– certain international services;
– public transport;
– certain supplies by charities;
– clothing and footwear for children or for protective purposes.

Exemption

Supplies in this category are regarded as not being subject to VAT at all. Any supplies made to the business which are attributable to such exempt supplies do not rank for input tax credit as described in question 94.

130

The more significant exempt supplies are as follows.
- sale or letting of land (with certain exceptions);
- insurance services;
- betting, gaming and lotteries;
- most financial services;
- education as provided at school or university;
- health and medical services;
- burial and cremation.

98   In what circumstances is my entitlement to reclaim VAT restricted?   ●

There are two situations where a registered trader may not be able to recover the whole of the input tax charged on goods and services supplied to him.

Non-deductible inputs

The VAT suffered on certain inputs is specifically defined as being non-deductible, so that it does not rank for credit under any circumstances. The costs presently within this exclusion are as follows.
1 Purchase of motor cars (except by motor traders), but not commercial vehicles. The exclusion does not apply to hiring or leasing charges nor to running costs.
2 Entertainment and hospitality (except for overseas customers and staff).
3 Expenditure on fixtures and fittings in a building of a kind not normally installed by a builder.
4 Expenditure other than for business purposes.

Partial exemption

As indicated in question 94, some restriction of input tax may be applicable where a business has a mixture of taxable (including zero rated) and exempt supplies. Many businesses are regularly in this situation, for example those in the property, construction or financial services fields. However, many other businesses, normally fully taxable, would find themselves treated as partly exempt by reason of the sale of a property or the receipt of rent or of bank deposit interest.

A fundamental principle of VAT is that input tax attributable to exempt outputs should not be recoverable. Where there is a mixture of taxable and exempt outputs, the input tax borne by the business should be apportioned between those categories of output on a reasonable basis. How this apportionment is made is a matter for agreement between the trader and C & E. Up to the present time, many arrangements have been agreed based on a specific attribution of inputs to taxable and exempt outputs, where it was possible to do this, with an allocation of the remaining deductible input tax pro rata between taxable and exempt outputs. Frequently, the whole of the input tax was allocated in this way in the interests of simplicity and convenience. There were also rules that enabled exempt outputs to be ignored if they were sufficiently small or incidental in relation to the business.

With effect from 1st April 1987, the existing rules relating to partial exemption are to be substantially modified. At the time of writing, the full extent of these changes has not been made clear by C & E, but it is known that a more specific attribution of inputs to taxable and exempt outputs will be required. The 'de minimus' and 'incidental' rules are also being amended.

The upshot of these changes is that any business with some, even small, exempt outputs may find that its ability to recover input tax is reduced. It may therefore need to take professional advice as to any arrangements that it can make to contain this reduction.

99 Is there any way I can plan to minimise the tax charge, and are there any special rules if my business is a company?

There is generally no way to minimise the actual tax charge whether your business is a company or a partnership or you are the sole proprietor.

It is important, however, that the VAT significance of transactions which the business intends to carry through is correctly understood, as any mistakes may be difficult to rectify after the event and can be expensive.

As the implications of VAT accounting are more connected with cash flow, if you are a trader who regularly claims a repayment you will be allowed to make a monthly return rather than the normal quarterly return. The actual format of your accounting records can give rise to planning considerations, for example, in the case of dealers in certain categories of second-hand goods, such as motor cars or works of art, where C & E regulations are particularly strict.

Similarly retailers who deal mainly in cash, and who do not normally issue tax invoices, have a choice of several schemes which are aimed at arriving at a calculated figure of output tax. If you are a retailer it is clearly important that you select the scheme most beneficial to you, so you should always take professional advice when setting up in business.

If your business is a company, generally it is taxed under the same rules as a sole trader or partnership. However, the one thing to remember is that if your company is a member of a group of companies it may be beneficial to be registered as a group and not as separate companies. The arrangements as to which companies are to be included and which are not operate very flexibly in practice.

100 Are there any situations where the VAT treatment needs to be specially considered?

There are a number of situations where, although there is no actual sale ('output' in the VAT jargon), tax has to be accounted for to C & E as if there had been one. The most notable of these are the following:

1 Where goods are supplied for non-business purposes, for example, for the private use of the proprietor of the business or of an employee.

2 Where goods are supplied by way of gift, even though for business purposes, and their cost is more than £10 (this includes a series of gifts of less than this amount to the same person where the total cost exceeds £10).

3 From the first VAT accounting period beginning after 6th April 1987, where petrol, supplied by the business, is used for private motoring by the proprietor or employees of the business. This is based on the scale of charges used for income tax purposes (see question 31), as follows:

Engine size	Quarterly scale £	Monthly scale £
Up to 1400cc	120 (15.65)	40 (5.22)
1400–2000cc	150 (19.56)	50 (6.52)
Over 2000cc	225 (29.34)	75 (9.78)

The amount of VAT is shown in brackets. The scale charges are reduced by 50% where the business mileage exceeds 4,500 a quarter (or 1,500 a month where monthly returns are made).

8 THE RANGE OF POSSIBILITIES

101 A final word

The present Government is committed to encouraging investment in businesses and to assist industries and areas where there are special problems. The existing *business opportunities programme* promoted by the Government is being widely publicised to ensure that everyone is aware of what schemes and assistance may be available.

The *Business Expansion Scheme* has already been described in question 61.

Another measure, the *Loan Guarantee Scheme,* was devised to help people to start in business and this was introduced in 1981. The Department of Industry, in conjunction with the major banks, will provide guarantees of up to 70% of the amounts advanced on approved ventures, up to a maximum of (currently) £75,000; interest is charged at a commercial rate with an additional premium to cover the guarantee.

In addition, there are also various incentives available in particular areas of business, for example the construction industry and agriculture, and in particular parts of the country, for example development areas and enterprise zones.

You will by now have realised that the title of this book is not quite true; the ways of saving tax are *not* limited to 101, for there are endless possibilities to be considered. Indeed, if you were to count the reliefs, allowances, pieces of advice and so on given in these 100 answers you would find they totalled well in excess of 101! However, you must remember that this book cannot supply you with *all* the answers–it can only draw your attention to matters to which more detailed care and attention should be given. Always seek professional advice on any taxation or other financial matter about which you are not clear.

APPENDICES

APPENDIX 1
RATES OF INCOME TAX 1986/87 and 1987/88

Rate %	1986/87 Band of taxable income £	Cumulative tax £	Rate %	1987/88 Band of taxable income £	Cumulative tax £
29	1 – 17,200	4,988	27	1 – 17,900	4,833
40	17,201 – 20,200	6,188	40	17,901 – 20,400	5,833
45	20,201 – 25,400	8,528	45	20,401 – 25,400	8,083
50	25,401 – 33,300	12,478	50	25,401 – 33,300	12,033
55	33,301 – 41,200	16,823	55	33,301 – 41,200	16,378
60	over 41,200	–	60	over 41,200	–

APPENDIX 2
PERSONAL ALLOWANCES 1986/87 and 1987/88

	1986/87 £	1987/88 £
Personal:		
single person	2,335	2,425
married man	3,655	3,795
Wife's earned income (maximum)	2,335	2,425
Age (see Note 1):		
age 65-80		
single person	2,850	2,960
married man	4,505	4,675
age over 80		
single person	2,850	3,070
married man	4,505	4,845
Housekeeper	100	100
Widow's bereavement allowance	1,320	1,370
Additional allowance for widows and others in respect of qualifying children	1,320	1,370
Dependent relative (see Note 2):		
single women etc.	145	145
others	100	100
Son's or daughter's services	55	55
Blind person (available to each qualifying spouse)	360	540
Life assurance (see Note 3): given by deduction at source	15%	15%

Notes

1 Excess over personal allowance withdrawn by £2 for every £3 of income over £9,800 (1986/87: £9,400).

2 Allowance reduced by excess of dependant's income over basic retirement pension.

3 Relief given only on policies in force on 13th March 1984. No relief allowed on policies entered into after that date.

APPENDIX 3
BENEFITS IN KIND–CARS AND CAR PETROL
1986/87 and 1987/88

| | Cars | | |
	Under 4 years old £	4 years old or more £	Car petrol £
1986/87			
Cars with original market value up to £19,250 and having a cylinder capacity:			
1300 cc or less	450	300	450
1301 cc – 1800 cc	575	380	575
over 1800 cc	900	600	900
Cars with original market value up to £19,250 and not having a cylinder capacity:			
less than £ 6,000	450	300	450
£6,000 – £ 8,499	575	380	575
£8,500 – £19,250	900	600	900
Cars with original market value over £19,250			
£19,251 – £29,000	1,320	875	900
over £29,000	2,100	1,400	900
1987/88			
Cars with original market value up to £19,250 and having a cylinder capacity:			
1400 cc or less	525	350	480
1401 cc – 2000 cc	700	470	600
over 2000 cc	1,100	725	900
Cars with original market value up to £19,250 and not having a cylinder capacity:			
less than £ 6,000	525	350	480
£6,000 – £ 8,499	700	470	600
£8,500 – £19,250	1,100	725	900
Cars with original market value of			
£19,250 – £29,000	1,450	970	900
over £29,000	2,300	1,530	900

APPENDIX 3 (continued)
BENEFITS IN KIND–CARS AND CAR PETROL
1986/87 and 1987/88

3 Where the car has only insubstantial business use (defined as less than 2,500 miles a year) or is an additional car provided by the employer the car benefit is increased by a half. There is no increase in the car petrol benefit.

4 The car petrol benefits only apply to cars made available by the employer; the normal benefit in kind legislation applies where petrol is provided by an employer for an individual's own car, hire car, etc.

5 From 6th April 1987, a VAT scale charge will be imposed where petrol is supplied by the business and is used for private journeys by the proprietor or employees of the business (see question 100).

Notes
1 Where there is preponderant business use (defined as more than 18,000 miles a year) both the car and car petrol benefits are reduced by a half.

2 Where the car is not available for a period of time (normally at least 30 consecutive days in a year), both the car and car petrol benefits are reduced proportionately.

APPENDIX 4
NATIONAL INSURANCE CONTRIBUTIONS 1986/87

	Employees %	*Employers* %
Class 1 employed		
Not contracted out – *on all earnings*		
up to £37.99 per week	Nil	Nil
up to £59.99 per week	5.00	5.00
up to £94.99 per week	7.00	7.00
up to £139.99 per week	9.00	9.00
up to £285 per week	9.00	10.45
on excess over £285 per week	Nil	10.45
Contracted out – *on all earnings*		
up to £37.99 per week	Nil	Nil
up to £59.99 per week		
on first £38	5.00	5.00
on balance	2.85	0.90
up to £94.99 per week		
on first £38	7.00	7.00
on balance	4.85	2.90
up to £139.99 per week		
on first £38	9.00	9.00
on balance	6.85	4.90
up to £285 per week		
on first £38	9.00	10.45
on balance	6.85	6.35
on excess over £285 per week	Nil	10.45

Classes 2 and 4 self-employed

Class 2 fixed per week
  no liability if earning below £2,075 per year   £3.75

Class 4 earnings related
  on profits between £4,450 and £14,820
  a year (see Note)   6.3%

Class 3 non-employed

Voluntary rate per week   £3.65

APPENDIX 4 (continued)
NATIONAL INSURANCE CONTRIBUTIONS 1987/88

	Employees %	Employers %
Class 1 employed		
Not contracted out – *on all earnings*		
up to £38.99 per week	Nil	Nil
up to £64.99 per week	5.00	5.00
up to £99.99 per week	7.00	7.00
up to £149.99 per week	9.00	9.00
up to £295 per week	9.00	10.45
on excess over £295 per week	Nil	10.45
Contracted out – *on all earnings*		
up to £38.99 per week	Nil	Nil
up to £64.99 per week		
on first £39	5.00	5.00
on balance	2.85	0.90
up to £99.99 per week		
on first £39	7.00	7.00
on balance	4.85	2.90
up to £149.99 per week		
on first £39	9.00	9.00
on balance	6.85	4.90
up to £295 per week		
on first £39	9.00	10.45
on balance	6.85	6.35
on excess over £295 per week	Nil	10.45

Classes 2 and 4 self-employed

Class 2 fixed per week
  no liability if earning below £2,125 per year — £3.85

Class 4 earnings related
  on profits between £4,590 and £15,340
  a year (see Note) — 6.3%

Class 3 non-employed

Voluntary rate per week — £3.75

Note
Half these contributions are allowable for income tax purposes.

101 Ways of Investing and Saving Money

If you are wondering how to make the most of your money, this straightforward handbook is designed to open your eyes to the myriad of investment opportunities available:

- **Banks and Building Societies**
- **Life Assurance and Pension Plans**
- **Stocks and Shares, Unit Trusts**
- **Property**
- **Small Businesses**
- **Precious metals, art and antiques**

This comprehensive guide to the wide range of savings and investment opportunities available assembles details of every conceivable form of investment. It covers 101 ways of investing money productively, from saving money with a bank or building society to buying wine, old cars, horses and, of course, stocks and shares.

101 Ways of Investing and Saving Money cuts through the financial jargon and examines the key issues enabling you to make the right decisions and reap the benefits in the future.

£2.50 net in UK

101 Ways to Run a Business Profitably

Setting up in business or already managing a small company? Here is a practical guide to running a successful operation which deals with all the major topics of concern to today's businessman:

- **How to forecast sales**
- **Methods of collecting money promptly**
- **How to assess a profit margin**
- **When to seek legal advice**
- **What to do about insurance and security obligations**
- **How to decide whether your business needs a computer**

101 Ways to Run a Business Profitably aims to help make your business – whatever its size – more successful and its future more secure. A team of management consultants from accountants Grant Thornton, under the editorship of senior consulting partner Gerald Nicholls and his colleagues, give straight-forward guidance on the key issues affecting profitability, drawing on their extensive knowledge and experience.

The team answers all the key questions that will help you realise your potential as a manager and improve the performance of your company.

£2.95 net in UK